Warm Up to Wool

Projects to Hook and Stitch

Martingale®
& COMPANY

Warm Up to Wool: Projects to Hook and Stitch
© 2004 by Martingale & Company

That Patchwork Place® is an
imprint of Martingale & Company®.

Martingale & Company
20205 144th Avenue NE
Woodinville, WA 98072-8478
www.martingale-pub.com

Printed in China
09 08 07 06 05 04   8 7 6 5 4 3 2 1

Library of Congress Cataloging-in-Publication Data

Warm up to wool : projects to hook and stitch /
[edited by Karen Costello Soltys].
      p. cm.
   ISBN 1-56477-520-8
 1. Rugs, Hooked. 2. Appliqué. 3. Wool. I. Soltys,
Karen Costello.
   TT850 .W37 2004
   746 . 7'4—dc22
                                   2003021772

Mission Statement

*Dedicated to providing quality products
and service to inspire creativity.*

Credits

President ◆ Nancy J. Martin
CEO ◆ Daniel J. Martin
Publisher ◆ Jane Hamada
Editorial Director ◆ Mary V. Green
Managing Editor ◆ Tina Cook
Editor ◆ Karen Costello Soltys
Copy Editor ◆ Tricia Toney
Design Director ◆ Stan Green
Illustrator ◆ Robin Strobel
Cover and Text Designer ◆ Regina Girard
Photographer ◆ Brent Kane

Special Thanks

*to Lynda Van Wyk for allowing us
to photograph the projects in this book
at the Speckled Hen Country Store.
Her charming shop is filled
to the brim with wonderful wools,
pottery, homespuns, and more.
For contact information, see page 95.*

Contents

Wonderful Wool

Long before I was a quilter and rug hooker, I loved making my own clothes. Wool skirts, slacks, and an occasional blazer were some of the most satisfying projects to make because wool was just so pleasant to work with. It's textural and tactile—and also quite forgiving. When I got hooked on quilting, I all but gave up garment making. (After all, I didn't have to worry about fitting, altering, or hemming!) But I never gave up my love of working with wool.

Today, I enjoy working by hand with wool fabrics, whether it be in the form of blanket-stitch appliqué or rug hooking. Both mediums are satisfying to my creative soul, and if working with wool is new to you, my hope is that you'll find just as much enjoyment right from your very first project.

Speaking of projects, seven fabulous designers or design teams have stitched and hooked such terrific projects for this book that you may have a hard time deciding which one to make first. I'm sure you'll be inspired by all of the artists' designs, color palettes, and techniques, which range in style from quite primitive to whimsical to more traditional. And you might be surprised to find that rug hooking and wool appliqué are not relegated only to making decorative table mats. While these items are fun to make to decorate your home and to give as gifts, you may want to try your hand at one of the other creative ideas in this book, such as a pillow, tote bag, or even an appliquéd lampshade.

If you're new to either wool appliqué or rug hooking, we'll help you get started with how-to information on both of these art forms. We review the tools and supplies you need, as well as the techniques you can use to make your projects a success. So don't hesitate. I encourage you to jump right in and try your hand at both of these time-honored crafts. The projects are easy to pick up and work on even if you have just small bits of time in your schedule, and the techniques don't take too long to master. What are you waiting for?

Karen Costello Soltys,
Editor

5

It All Starts with Wool

All of the projects in this book are made predominantly of wool. So where do you find it, and how do you make it ready to stitch or hook? Those are the questions we'll answer in this section.

New Wool, Old Wool

If you're lucky enough to live by a quilt shop or fabric store that carries new wool on the bolt—good for you! You already have a ready source of wool. If you don't have such a shop within driving distance, you can find new wool online or from many of the resources listed on page 95.

Another source of wool is vintage wool. You have to be willing to spend a little time to search for wool garments, yardage, or blankets at thrift shops and yard sales, but sometimes you can find just the color you need for your project. It requires some effort to tear out the seams of garments, but if the color and texture are right, it can be worth your trouble.

With either new wool or old wool, the key is buying the right weight of wool, and washing and drying it to shrink it slightly before beginning your project. Avoid gabardines and other slick or lightweight wool. Even after shrinking or felting, they're just too limp to work with. They may be great for a new spring skirt, but not so hot for wool appliqué or rug hooking.

Instead, look for wool that has a little more substance to it. Blanket weight is too heavy for rug hooking, but it can be perfect for the background of a penny rug. For appliqué shapes and rug-hooking strips, however, a nice midweight wool will work best. As an example, the kind of wool used to make a nice plaid skirt or men's wool shirt is perfect. And that goes for buying new wool off the bolt as well as for thrift shopping. It's only a bargain if you can use the wool in the end. Even if a skirt costs two dollars, you've merely wasted two dollars if the wool is too wimpy and frays readily.

Preparing Wool

Whether you start with new wool right off the bolt, vintage wool, or a mix, the first thing you need to do is wash your fabric. The wool needs to shrink a little (but not become too thick or felted) in order to give it the perfect texture for your project.

Wash the wool in your washing machine with a bit of detergent and hot water. Do not use fabric softener. Set the rinse cycle to cold. This change in temperature causes the wool to shrink. If the wool you're starting with is already fairly heavy, you may want to wash it in warm water to prevent too much shrinking. After the final rinse cycle, toss the wool in the dryer. Optimally, you'd like it to be damp-dry upon removal. You can lay it flat until it's completely dry. Overdrying in the dryer can cause wrinkles to set in, and they can be very hard to remove. Once it's completely dry, fold or roll wool yardage and store it to prevent unnecessary wrinkling.

If you have some vintage garments in the mix, after the initial washing, you'll need to rip apart the seams, remove buttons, hems, plackets, and the like. Then it's a good idea to wash the wool again to get any dust and lint out of the seam areas and to close up the tiny holes made by the stitching. Dry as before, fold, and store.

No Moths Allowed

If you do purchase or scavenge for used wool garments, you should always wash them immediately upon bringing them into your house. You can wait until later to rip them apart and do the second washing, but you never know if you're inadvertently bringing in unwanted creatures on old wool clothing. If you find a bargain but don't have time to wash it, leave it in the trunk of your car until you're ready to launder it.

A Note about Overdyeing Wool

Some of the projects in this book use new wool, right off the bolt in rich or bright colors. In some situations, that's just the look you want. Other times, you may want colors that are subtle or plaids that look a bit more blended than you're able to find. In that case, you can overdye the fabrics. You'll find quite a few books on the subject, complete with instructions and dye recipes for a wide variety of colors.

An easy, low-cost way to subdue the color of your wool is to put several pieces of wool that are in the same color family together in a pot of water and boil them on top of your stove. After the water reaches a rolling boil, turn the heat off and let the fabrics sit in the water overnight. Some of the dye will bleed out of the fabrics during the boiling process. The various colors will mix in the water and seep back into the fabrics as the water becomes cooler. All the fabrics in your pot will look similar to one another, each individual color more subtle than before.

These days, more and more quilt and craft shops are carrying wools for penny rugs and hooked rugs, and you may be able to find the off-the-bolt and hand-dyed colors you need.

Penny Rug Appliqué

If you're new to wool appliqué, making your first penny rug will be a treat. The whole process is fairly quick and easy. You don't need very many tools or supplies, and once your shapes are prepared, your project is even portable. If you're familiar with traditional appliqué, you'll be surprised at how easy it is to make the assorted shapes and stitch them in place. After all, there are no seam allowances to worry about turning under. And the blanket stitch, which is traditionally used to hold the shapes in place, is much quicker to do than traditional hand appliqué.

Tools and Supplies

In addition to the wool for your project, you may already have everything else you need in your sewing room or kitchen!

Template Materials

The easiest way to make patterns for wool appliqué is to trace the pattern onto freezer paper and then use that pattern to cut out the wool shapes. You can find freezer paper at most grocery stores in the same aisle where the plastic wraps and aluminum foil are displayed. If your pattern has a lot of repeated shapes in it, you may also want to have some template plastic on hand. That way you can trace the shape once onto the plastic and then use the template to make multiple copies of the pattern on freezer paper.

Some of the project designers recommend using fusible web rather than freezer paper to make patterns so that you can fuse the pieces in place for pin-free stitching.

A black fine-point permanent marker is also a vital item. It's good for tracing patterns onto template plastic, freezer paper, and fusible web. You'll want one (or more) of these in your sewing kit.

Scissors

Regular fabric shears are good for cutting out larger pieces, such as the background piece and any of the larger appliqués. You may find smaller scissors easier to control for cutting smaller, detailed shapes. In addition, you'll need embroidery scissors or thread snips for hand-sewing purposes.

Needles and Threads

Look for larger hand-sewing needles, such as size 20 or 22 chenille needles. Tapestry needles work well, but make sure the point isn't too blunt to go through your wool. The key thing is that the eye is large enough to fit two strands of floss or a single strand of pearl cotton.

Everyone seems to have her (or his) personal favorite when it comes to thread for penny rugs. Embroidery floss comes in the largest variety of colors, so if you're looking for a perfect match, floss may be for you. Floss is six-stranded cotton thread, packaged in skeins. For appliqué, you need two strands at a time. Simply cut your thread to length and then peel off the strands you need.

Pearl cotton is a twisted thread and is also sold in skeins as well as balls. It comes in various weights or thicknesses: size 3, 5, 8, and 12. Size 3 is the thickest; size 12 is the finest. For blanket-stitching, size 8 works well. If you're working on a large piece with chunky shapes, then you may be able to use size 5. Pearl cotton tends to show up a little more than floss because the thread is round rather than flat; however, it is available in fewer colors than floss.

Some folks like to use other threads for their work, including wool floss and topstitching thread. Wool floss can add a nice dimension to your work, but work with short lengths, as it can fray if it gets too much wear at the eye of the needle as you pull the needle in and out of the fabric. Topstitching thread or linen thread may be used for a rustic look. Depending on how heavy the thread is, you may need to use more than one strand at a time.

Basting Supplies

To hold the wool appliqués in place, you may either pin them or adhere them another way. Everyone has pins, so this may be the best option for you. If you

You don't need much more than wool fabric, pearl cotton or floss, pins, needles, and a pair of sharp scissors to make a wool appliqué project.

find that the pins are getting in the way and snagging your thread, you may want to look for another option.

Some stitchers prefer to use a spray adhesive on the back of their pieces. You can stick the pieces in place where you want them, without the use of pins. Another "sticky" option is to use a fabric glue stick. A daub from a glue stick on the back of your appliqués should be enough to hold the appliqués in place until they are secured with stitching. Liquid fabric glue isn't a good option, however, as it dries hard and will show up in your finished work by darkening the fabric.

Staple Basting

For a really secure hold, and one that won't hamper your stitching, try stapling the appliqués in place. Staples don't have sharp tips sticking out to grab your thread, and they're really handy, especially if you plan to transport your project. You can be sure those pieces won't fall off! To remove the staples when you're through, simply lift them off with the type of staple remover that looks like a letter opener, rather than the spring-loaded claw type of remover.

Making Templates

Some shapes, such as vines or stripes, can be cut without templates. You can simply cut a straight strip of fabric and appliqué it in place. Even if the vine is to be curved, you can still use a strip of fabric cut on the straight of grain because the wool is flexible enough to bend into gentle curves. Other shapes will require templates, and you can trace the pattern from the book directly onto freezer paper if you like. Or, if you'll need multiple pieces of a pattern, it's a good idea to make a plastic template first.

1. Trace the pattern onto the template plastic and cut out the shape on the drawn line.

2. Trace around the plastic template onto the dull (non-coated) side of the freezer paper as many times as needed. (While you can get away with reusing freezer-paper shapes for cotton appliqué, it's a good idea to make one template for each piece needed when working with wool. When you peel the paper off the wool, you'll see that quite a bit of fuzz sticks to the paper, making it hard to adhere it to the wool a second or third time.)

3. Cut out the freezer-paper shapes about ¼" outside of the drawn lines.

Preparing Appliqués

Getting your appliqué shapes ready for your penny rug is quite easy. You can use either side of the wool, whichever you prefer. The edges are left raw and won't fray due to the felting process, so you don't need to allow extra fabric for a seam allowance or turn under the edges as you stitch. And you don't have to worry about grain line, either. You can cut shapes in any direction, to make the best use of your fabric. If you want plaids or checks to run diagonally across the appliqué, cut them that way. If you want to take advantage of dark or light shading in a hand-dyed wool, place the templates accordingly. It's just about impossible to go wrong.

1. Decide which side of the wool you want to use and then press the freezer-paper templates shiny side down onto your selected right side of the wool.

2. Cut out each shape, cutting directly on the lines. Peel the paper off the wool. (You may want to leave the patterns in place until you're ready to appliqué.)

3. Secure the pieces in place on the background or on top of whatever other shape they will be appliquéd to. You can use pins, a glue stick, or spray adhesive to hold the shapes in place.

Using Fusible Patterns

If you prefer, you can follow the steps above to make your patterns from paper-backed fusible web rather than freezer paper. It's not necessary to have the shapes glued to the background, but some people find that with small shapes (those too small for pin basting), the fusible web is a handy way to hold the pieces in place while you stitch them.

Stitching Techniques

In simpler patterns, a shape is appliquéd directly onto the background fabric. In some of the more complex designs, the appliqué shapes are layered, one on top of another. In that case, appliqué the topmost piece onto the piece below it, and then attach the whole unit to the background. This way, you'll never be appliquéing through more than one underneath layer, and you'll always have a place to hide your starting and stopping knots.

Most of the appliqué projects in the book use blanket-stitch appliqué. However, some of the more primitive-looking projects use more of a whipstitch, which is a little less elaborate. Other stitch details are also used to embellish some of the projects.

Blanket Stitch

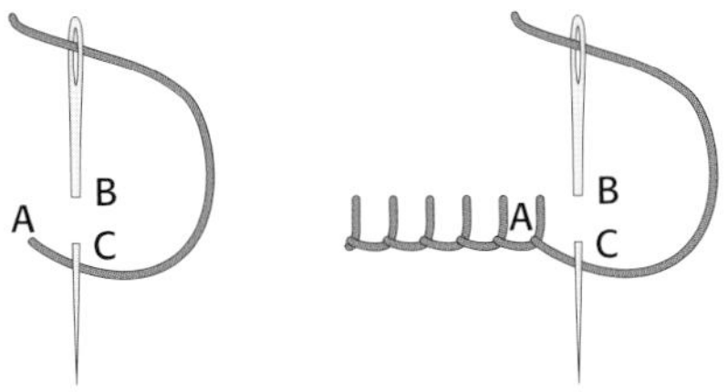

Chain Stitch

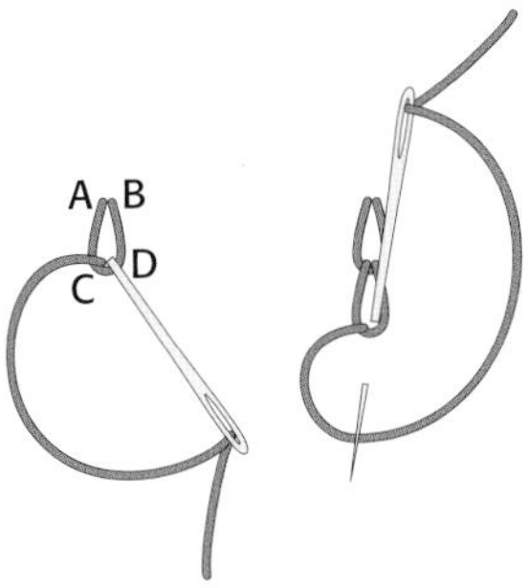

French Knot

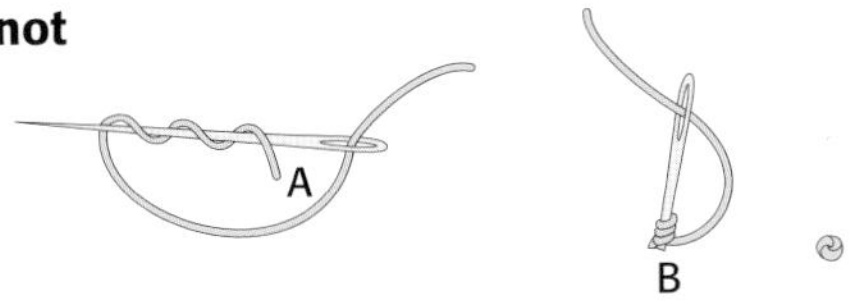

Outline Stitch

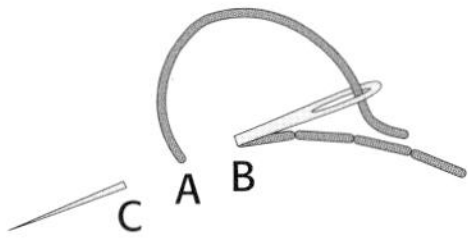

Running Stitch

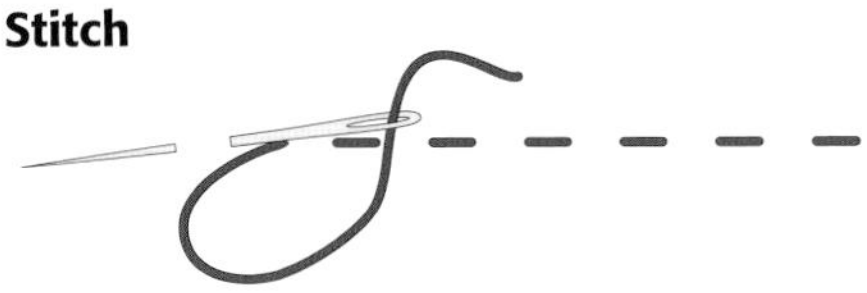

Whipstitch

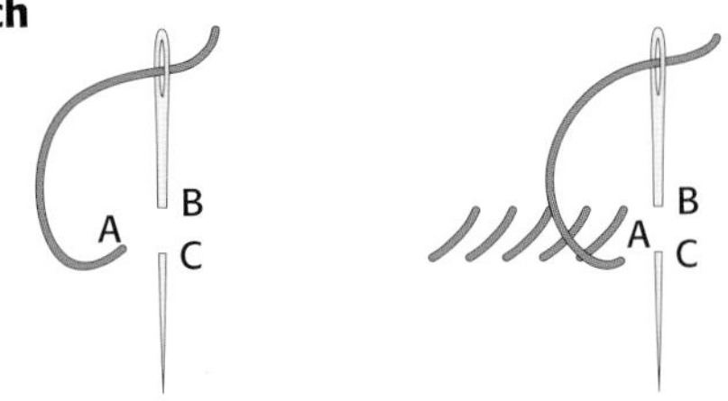

Caring for Your Penny Rug

Projects stitched in wool need very little in the way of maintenance. You don't need to (and really shouldn't) press the completed rug. You don't want to flatten the wool or put sheen on it. If you fold it for storage, you may find that it needs a bit of pressing to get out a crease. Try steaming it from the wrong side, holding your iron above the fabric. If this isn't enough, you can place a damp towel on the wrong side of the penny rug and press.

Don't wash your penny rug either by hand or machine, and don't dry-clean it. If something is spilled on it, use a damp cloth or sponge to mop up the liquid. You'll find that wool is very resilient, and spills should bead up on the wool rather than soak right in. To remove dust or pet hair, you can shake out the rug or use a lint brush or roller. (The masking tape variety works especially well.)

5¢ Rescue

If you should happen to iron a shiny spot onto your wool, try this inexpensive and clever trick to eliminate the shine. Rub the edge of a U.S. nickel (not a dime or a quarter) over the shiny spot to bring the fabric back to life.

The Ins and Outs of Rug Hooking

Like wool appliqué, rug hooking is a fun craft that is easy to learn. Before you can start hooking, you'll need to transfer your pattern or design onto your desired rug backing fabric and cut the wool you plan to use into strips. Let's look first at the supplies you'll need, and then we can get hooking.

Tools and Supplies

You don't need many tools, although you'll find there are a wide variety of choices available to you. If you have a quilting hoop and a rotary cutter, all you need is a rug hook, a piece of rug backing fabric, and wool, and you can get started.

Backing Fabrics

Most rugs today are hooked into one of three types of fabric: Scottish burlap, monk's cloth, or linen. What these fabrics have in common is a regular, open weave that allows you to fit a hook through the fabric and stay on-grain. Scottish burlap is the least expensive choice, but it is also the roughest of the three fabrics. Traditionally, rugs were hooked into burlap feed sacks, and that fabric remains a popular choice today.

Monk's cloth is a much softer, flexible fabric. You might find it in craft shops, but be sure to choose the variety with smaller openings for rug hooking rather than the type with a large open weave for afghan making.

Finally, there is linen. This is the most expensive option, but has a nice hand and is easy to hook on. Many rug hookers start out working with burlap because it's readily available, and is most often used in small kits. If you find burlap to be too scratchy, you may want to opt for either monk's cloth or linen.

If you can't find these fabrics at your local quilt or fabric shop, you can buy them via mail or the Internet. See "Resources" on page 95.

Transfer Supplies

You'll need to get your desired pattern onto the backing fabric. Complete instructions for doing that are given in "Transfer the Pattern" on page 14. Here, we'll just review the supplies you need for transferring.

- **Full-size pattern.** Most of the patterns in the book have been reduced to fit onto a book page. You'll need to enlarge the pattern to the actual size needed, either with a photocopier that makes enlargements or by hand. If enlarging by hand, you'll need paper large enough to fit the complete design.

- **Red Dot Tracer or craft netting.** To transfer the design onto the backing fabric, you'll need to make a copy of the pattern that you can then trace over to transfer the ink onto the rug backing fabric. Red Dot Tracer is like nonwoven interfacing with red dots marked at 1" intervals. It's permeable, so when you trace over it with a permanent marker, the ink will seep through onto the backing fabric. Likewise, craft netting or tulle has an open weave that lets you see through to the original pattern and allows the ink to flow through the openings to mark the backing fabric. Either of these options can be found in fabric stores and are quite inexpensive.

- **Indelible fine-point marker.** This is needed to transfer the design onto the backing fabric. Make sure the marker is permanent so that once the ink is dry, it won't rub off onto your wool as you hook.

- **Masking tape.** To transfer a pattern accurately, you'll need to tape the backing fabric in place, as well as tape the pattern in place on top of the fabric. Regular masking tape and blue painter's tape work equally well.

Hooks

If you've ever bought a rug-hooking kit, chances are it came with a rug hook. These hooks are inexpensive and do the trick. At some point you may want to upgrade to a different style handle, or even a different shape hook. So many choices are available to you! Short, rounded ball handles; long, pencil-type handles; and midsize ergonomic handles each have their devotees. If you have a shop nearby where you can try them out, you're in luck. If not, you can find all sorts

A frame with needle-gripper strips will hold your project securely as you hook; however, you can substitute a quilting hoop for holding your rug taut. Likewise, a strip cutter makes quick work of cutting strips, but a rotary cutter and ruler can do the trick, too.

of hooks available on the Internet. Prices range from about $5 to $30, depending on the type of wood used and the style of the hook.

Most of the projects in this book use wider cuts of wool, so a "primitive" hook with a "medium" shaft will work well. Hooks for "traditional" rug hooking have much finer shafts that can't handle the wider cuts of wool.

Hoops and Frames

It's important that your backing fabric be held taut when hooking to get uniform loops and coverage. You can either put your fabric in a quilt hoop or on a rug-hooking frame. If you already own a quilt hoop, you might want to start with that. A 14" hoop works well, as you can fit a fairly large hooking area inside the hoop, yet it isn't so large as to be unwieldy. You can also use a hoop on a tabletop or floor stand, if you have one. One nice benefit of working in a hoop is that you can easily rotate it as needed to change your hooking direction. If your hoop on a stand swivels, you'll find that to be a practical feature.

Unlike round quilting hoops, rug-hooking frames are generally rectangular. Many styles are available, but they all have a similar feature: needle-gripper strips to hold your work securely. Prices vary widely on frames, depending on whether they swivel, tilt, collapse for storage, or have tightening ratchets. The choice of frame or hoop is strictly personal, so try out various types before buying if you can.

Strip Cutter or Rotary Cutter

The last item you'll need for rug hooking is a tool for cutting your strips. Traditionally, strips were torn or cut with scissors. Today, most rug hookers cut their wool strips with a strip cutter. These gadgets let you cut two or more strips at once by cranking the handle to feed the wool through the blades. They make quick work of cutting strips on grain, but again, they require an investment, ranging from about $140 to $400. Rest assured, you do not need a strip cutter to make a hooked rug, although they are very handy. You can use a rotary cutter, mat, and ruler used for quiltmaking (which you probably already own), or you can even buy wool that has been precut into strips for you.

Getting Started

Okay, let's get started. The first thing you need to do is prepare your backing fabric. You'll need to do something to the edges of the fabric to prevent them from fraying as you work on your rug. And you'll need to transfer the design to your rug. You'll also need to decide how you want to finish your rug—with binding tape, by whipping the edges with yarn, or another method—before you start to hook, because some methods require up-front preparation. For more details, see "Finishing Details" on page 18.

Prepare the Backing Fabric

First, determine how big your project design area is. Then add about 8" to each dimension if you'll be hooking on a frame or 16" if you'll be hooking in a hoop. Cut your backing fabric to your calculated size. For instance, if your finished rug will be 12" x 18", cut your backing fabric 20" x 26" for hooking on a frame; cut it 28" x 34" for hooking in a hoop.

After cutting your backing fabric to size, you'll need to finish the edges so they won't fray. If you have

a serger, you can quickly and easily serge the edges. Another option is to zigzag them on your regular sewing machine. If neither of these ideas appeal to you, you can fold a strip of masking tape over each edge, encasing the loose fibers.

Transfer the Pattern

Most rug-hooking patterns are sold as a design already transferred to the backing fabric. Some designers offer you a choice of background fabric (linen, burlap, or monk's cloth). To use the patterns in this book, or to create your own patterns, you'll need to transfer the design onto the backing fabric yourself. It's not hard to do, and it's a good skill to know because then you'll have the flexibility of making printed patterns any size you want and the freedom to design your own rugs. Transferring the pattern requires just a few steps.

1. If necessary, enlarge the pattern to the desired size. The patterns in this book all list the percentage you'll need to enlarge them to make rugs the same size as the ones pictured. You can enlarge them yourself on a photocopier, take them to a copy shop and have them enlarged for you (a good option for patterns that need to be enlarged more

than 200%), or you can enlarge them by hand, following the grid printed behind each pattern.

2. Tape the full-size paper pattern to a large flat surface such as a table or floor (wood or vinyl, not carpeted). Lay your Red Dot Tracer or craft netting over the pattern, smooth it out, and tape it in place.

3. Using a permanent fine-point marker, trace over every line in the printed pattern. You can use a ruler to help guide you along straight lines, such as borders, if desired. Lift the Red Dot Tracer or netting from the pattern and check to make sure that all lines have been copied.

4. Tape your prepared backing fabric onto the same large flat surface. Make sure the grain lines are straight and that there are no creases or wrinkles in the fabric. Lay the Red Dot Tracer or netting pattern over the backing fabric, centering the pattern over the fabric and making sure that the outer edges of the design are aligned with the straight grain of the fabric. If you don't align the pattern with the fabric grain, your rug will tend to twist out of shape as you work on it. Tape the pattern in place securely.

5. Using your permanent marker, trace over the Red Dot Tracer or netting pattern again. This time, the tracings will go through the pattern to mark the design onto the backing fabric. Before removing the pattern completely, lift up one corner and check the backing fabric to make sure that all parts of the design have been marked. Fill in any missing lines and then remove the pattern from the backing fabric.

Decide on a Finishing Technique

It's a good idea to plan ahead and know what method you'd like to use for finishing your rug before you begin. That's because some of the finishing techniques are easier to do if you start them before you begin to hook. If you want to use rug-binding tape, for instance, it's quicker and easier if you sew it to the rug backing before you have hooked loops in the way. Other techniques can be started and completed after all hooking is complete.

Cut the Strips

Once you've decided on your color scheme and gathered your wool, you'll need to cut the wool into strips. You'll need wool that's about four to six times larger than the area to be covered, so plan accordingly. You don't need to cut all your strips at once, and perhaps it's better if you don't. They tend to get tangled and if you don't use all the strips, it's hard to determine how much wool you have once it is cut. If you plan to use a variety of wools, such as three or four different reds, cut some strips from each wool so you can mix up the strips as you hook.

Each project in the book tells you what size to cut the strips. Most are size 8, but some do call for narrower strips, so be sure to read the directions before you cut anything. In rug hooking, strips are given as whole-number sizes, size 3 through size 9 or 10. (These numbers are short for the number of thirty-seconds of an inch needed for the width of each strip.) For instance, size 8 is $8/32$" or $1/4$" wide. Size 6 is $6/32$" or $3/16$" wide. If you use a strip cutter, you simply attach the size blade required and your strips will be cut uniformly to that size. If you use a rotary cutter, you'll find it's easier to cut size 8 or $1/4$"-wide strips than it is to do narrower ones. If you need size 6 strips, you can start by cutting strips $3/8$" wide and then snipping one end of the strip in the center and tearing it into two narrower strips.

Stay on Grain

Make sure to always cut the wool strips on grain. Because the strips are narrow, if they are cut slightly off grain, they tend to fray or tear apart as you pull them through the backing fabric. To make sure you're working on grain, make a snip at one end of the wool and then tear a narrow piece of wool away from the main piece. Wool will always tear on the grain, so now you know you have a perfectly straight edge that is on grain.

The Hooking Technique

The basic hooking technique is easy to master. First, we'll review how to hook, and then give pointers for the best order in which to hook and how to change direction.

Starting and Stopping

To begin, load your backing fabric into your hoop or onto your frame. Make sure the backing fabric is taut and not skewed. The weave of the fabric should look nice and square. Now, hold your hook in your dominant hand and a strip between the thumb and forefinger of your other hand. (Our diagrams show right-handed hooking, but you can just as easily hook left-handed.)

1. Push the tip of the hook through a hole in the backing fabric, hook it around the wool strip, and pull up the short end. You need a wool tail of about ½" to 1" showing above the backing fabric. If you've pulled up more than this, simply tug on the strip from beneath the backing fabric to adjust the tail length.

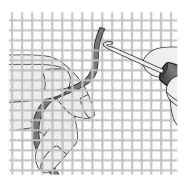

2. Holding the strip from beneath the backing fabric, poke the hook through next hole in the backing fabric and pull up a loop. The loops should be roughly the same height as the width of the strip. It is often easier to pull the loop up a little higher

than necessary, and then gently pull from underneath until the loop is at your desired height.

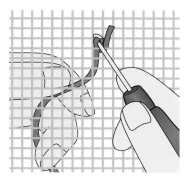

3. Continue hooking loops in this manner, following the grid of the backing fabric. Depending on how wide your strips are, you will need to skip a hole between each loop or after every second or third loop. The goal is to have the loops touch one another so that you can't see through to the backing fabric, but to not pack them so tightly together that they crush one another. It's common for beginners to hook the loops too close together, which will make it nearly impossible for the finished rug to lie flat.

4. When you reach the end of a strip or you need to end the color you're working with, pull the tail up through the top of the fabric. Again, leave about ½" to 1", and clip off the rest of the strip. The tails will be clipped off later, so they will be even with the height of the loops. To start a new strip, pull up the tail as before, this time pulling it up through the same hole as your ending tail. Continue hooking as before.

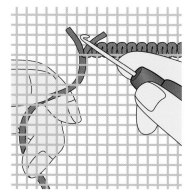

5. When all the area around the beginning and ending tails has been hooked, you can trim the tails so that they are even with the surrounding loops. Hold your scissors parallel to the rug surface with the blades even with the loops. Snip the tails off and notice how "invisible" these tail ends become.

Avoid Side-by-Side Tails

While you start a new strip in the same hole where the last one ended, it's not a good idea to have too many tails in the same area. The starting and stopping tails fill in a space as well as a loop, but they aren't rounded on top. If the starting and stopping points start lining up side by side from one row to the next, these spots will be noticeable in the finished rug.

If you're running out of a strip, and it's bound to end exactly next to where you ended in the previous row of hooking, simply stop hooking with that strip early, snip off the excess length, and start with a new strip. Your rug will look more professional, even if you had to waste a bit of one strip.

Another place to avoid starting and stopping is at the corner of a border. Snipped-off tails at these locations will also be more noticeable. It's best if you can turn the corner using a single strip, and then start a new one somewhere along the straightaway.

Hooking Direction

Now that you've practiced hooking in a straight line, it's time to get a little more creative. Depending on the pattern you choose, you may need to hook in circles, swirls, or in different directions.

It is possible to learn to hook in any direction, although hooking toward yourself is usually the most comfortable position. No matter what direction you hook in, the goal is to keep the wool strip on the underside of the rug flat and untwisted. By turning the angle of your hook slightly, you can make loops that start to turn a corner. If you find this hard to do, you can simply turn your hoop slightly so that you're still hooking toward yourself. If you're working on a frame, you can turn the frame, or simply lift your work from the gripper strips and reposition it. This way you can hook completely around a circle or make gentle curves.

Swirls in the background can suggest a windy day.

If you need to turn a corner, however, you may want to end the strip and start with a new one, working in the new direction. You don't want to twist the strip underneath the rug, or carry the strip over other parts that have already been hooked. This will put more wear and tear on the strips and shorten the life of your rug.

Hooking Order

It's a good idea to come up with a plan for what to hook first and what to save for last. The projects in this book all specify a logical hooking sequence, but there are some basic rules of thumb to follow for any pattern you decide to hook.

1. If there are any grid lines in your rug, such as in "Hooked Penny Rug" on page 92, hook those first so you can be sure that you're hooking on-grain.

2. Hook the row that separates the border from the interior of the rug. Taking care of these lines now assures that they will be hooked on-grain and that you don't have to make room to squeeze them in later.

3. Hook motifs starting in the center of the rug and work outward. For primitive-style hooking, shapes are often outlined first (in matching or contrasting wool) and then filled in. Hook the outline just inside the drawn lines; otherwise, your shapes will turn out too large.

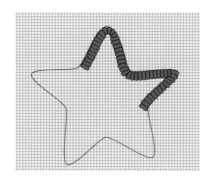

Hook inside the drawn lines.

4. Hook the border next to make sure it is all on-grain.

5. Fill in the background last. If desired, you could hook a row or two around the motifs as you're working on the rug to make sure you are satisfied with your background color choices. However, it's a good idea to complete the border before filling in the background area completely. Depending on the look you want, you can hook the background back and forth in rows, or you can follow the outlines of the motifs and even add swirling lines in large open parts of the background for additional interest.

Finishing Details

As mentioned earlier, you have several options when it comes to binding or finishing your rug. And as you'll see later, many of the projects in this book are finished in different fashions. When it comes to making any of the rugs, you can select the method you like best. You don't need to finish your rug in the same manner as shown on the original project.

Blocking

When your rug is completely hooked, you may notice that it's not completely square. Sometimes, from pulling it taut in the hoop or frame, it can become a little misshapen. That's where blocking comes in.

To block your rug, tug on the backing fabric to pull it back into shape. Then lay it right side down on your ironing board or another firm, flat surface. Cover it with a damp towel, and then press it with an iron set for steam. Do not iron back and forth, but rather stamp the iron up and down, using firm pressure. Press the entire piece, and then turn the rug over and repeat the stamping process. The steam will shrink the wool and give a smooth appearance to your finished rug, helping to hide any uneven loops. Remove the towel and allow the rug to dry flat overnight or until it is completely dry.

Rug-Binding Tape

One common method for finishing a rug is to use purchased twill tape and attach it to the outer perimeter of the design. When the rug is completed, the tape is folded to the wrong side of the rug and whipstitched in place. Preshrink the tape by soaking it in warm water and allowing it to dry before using.

Purchase enough rug-binding tape to go completely around the perimeter of your design, plus several extra inches for turning the corners, overlapping at the ends, and shrinkage. If you want to attach the tape by machine, it's best to do this prior to hooking your rug so that you can stitch it right up to the edge of the design. Once you've hooked the loops, it will be impossible to sew closely to the edge because of the bulk of the loops. Of course you can still choose this option for rugs that have already been hooked.

You'll simply need to sew the binding tape to the rug by hand.

1. On your rug backing, draw a line ⅛" outside of the border, using a ruler if your rug has straight edges. (You may need to "eyeball" curved edges.)

2. Lay the binding tape on top of the backing fabric so the tape overlaps the design area, and the edge is aligned with the drawn line. Pin in place. Fold about 1" of the starting end back over itself so that the raw edge won't show once the binding is complete.

   When you come to a corner, you will need to pleat the tape so that you can turn the corner. This pleat will give you enough ease with the tape to turn it to the backside of the rug when hooking is complete.

3. Stitch the tape in place, stitching ⅛" from the edge of the tape and overlapping the ends of the tape.

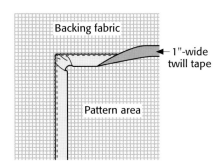

4. Fold the tape back away from the design area and baste it in place to hold it out of your way for hooking.

5. After all hooking is complete, trim the excess backing fabric, leaving about 1" of backing that will be covered with the twill tape. Cut the corners at an angle to reduce bulk. Then fold the tape and the excess backing to the wrong side of the rug. Fold a miter at each corner and pin in place. Whipstitch the edge of the tape in place on the back of the rug.

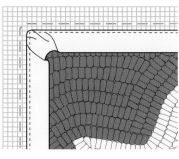

Trim.

Self Finish

Two of the rugs in this book (Heart Quartet on page 28 and Hooked Penny Rug on page 92) do not use binding tape or any other materials for finishing the edge of the rug. They simply have the backing fabric folded to the back of the rug and whipstitched in place.

1. Draw a line 2" away from the last row of hooking on all sides of the rug.

2. Cut away the excess backing fabric along your marked lines. Trim off the corners.

3. Zigzag stitch the edges or use a serger to finish the edges to prevent them from fraying.

4. Turn the unhooked backing fabric to the back of the rug. Fold miters at the corners and pin in place.

5. Whipstitch the raw edge of the foundation to the back of the rug. Make sure to stitch into the foundation fabric and not just the loops.

6. If desired, you can use a permanent marker to darken the edges of the foundation if they show around the edge of the rug from the right side.

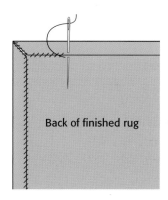

Back of finished rug

Whipstitching with Yarn

A popular finish for primitive rugs is to whipstitch the edges with wool yarn that matches or coordinates with your rug border. This can be done as a flat finish as described below, or the backing can be filled with cording to round the edges, as explained in "Whipstitching over Cording," below right. You will need 100%-wool yarn, such as 3-ply tapestry yarn, or worsted-weight knitting yarn, and a large-eye needle for the yarn.

1. Mark a line 1" away from the last row of hooking on all sides of the rug.

2. Zigzag stitch along the marked lines, and then trim the excess backing fabric away, just outside of the zigzag stitching.

3. Fold the rug backing fabric toward the front of the rug, so that the raw edge just meets the last row of loops. Fold again in the same manner, so that the folded edge is approximately ¼" to ⅜" wide. If desired, you can use quilting thread to baste the folds in place so that you won't have to hold them as you whipstitch with yarn.

4. At the corners, you can trim some of the excess fabric off at an angle to reduce bulk. Then fold the fabric toward the right side of the rug, folding each side in at the corner to form a miter. Baste in place.

5. Using two or three plies of yarn and a large-eye tapestry needle, whipstitch the yarn around the folded backing fabric. To start, bring the needle up from the back of the rug, right at the edge of the loops. Leave a 2" tail of yarn. Then simply wrap the yarn around the folded edge and stick the needle up through the back of the rug, right next to the first stitch. As you continue to make stitches, make sure they cover the yarn tail. Continue sewing in this manner, whipping the wool around the binding until the entire fold of backing fabric has been covered.

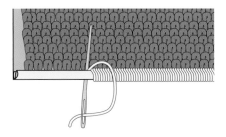

6. To end each length of yarn, simply slide the needle back about 1" through the stitches you've already taken. Bring the needle up and snip off the excess yarn.

Color Options

If you have dyed your own wools for your project, you may want to consider dyeing the whipping yarn to match. As long as you use 100%-wool yarn (tapestry yarn or worsted-weight knitting yarn), the yarn will take the dyes just as well as the wool fabric does. Another option is to use pre-dyed colors, but to mix them up. Cut yarn into about 18" lengths and pull the plies apart. Choose one ply each of three different colors to stitch with at one time to give a heathered look to your rug finish.

Whipstitching over Cording

This finishing method is similar to whipstitching without cording, although it does require the extra step of adding twill tape. It makes a nice, firm edge around the rug, which will be about the same height as the hooked loops. The finish is durable, and thus a good choice for rugs that will be used on the floor.

For this method, you will need 100%-wool yarn and a large-eye tapestry needle for whipping, quilting thread for sewing, ¼"- or ⅜"-diameter cotton cording (used for corded edges in pillows and upholstery), and twill rug-binding tape. Allow enough tape and cording to go around the perimeter of your rug, plus some extra for shrinking. Soak the tape and cording in warm water and allow to air-dry before using them.

1. Mark a line 1¼" outside of the last row of hooking on all sides of the rug.

2. Zigzag stitch along the marked lines, and then trim the excess backing fabric away, just outside of the zigzag stitching.

3. Lay your project right side down on the table and place the preshrunk cotton cording along the outside edge of your hooking. Roll the edge of the backing fabric toward you over the cording and pin it in place all around the perimeter of the rug.

4. Turn the rug so it is right side up. You should see a small width of the background fabric wrapped neatly over the cording around the entire project, just as piping goes around a pillow. Using quilting thread, hand sew basting stitches through both layers of the unhooked rug backing fabric to encase the cording. Remove the pins as you go. Be careful not to catch the wool loops as you baste.

5. Thread a tapestry needle with three plies of wool yarn, each ply about 18" to 24" long. Insert the needle through the back of the project through both layers of backing fabric. Leave a 2" tail of yarn on the back side of the project.

6. Working from left to right, bring the wool yarn up and over the cording and enter the needle directly next to the original starting point on the back, making sure that you are beginning to hide the yarn tail with the whipstitches. Continue stitching in this manner, until you are nearing the end of your yarn strand. Bring the yarn to the back of the rug and weave the needle under the whipstitches to hide the tail of yarn. Snip off any excess. Begin again with a new strand, hiding the tails and whipstitching as before.

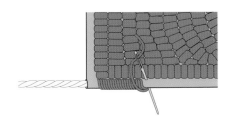

7. When you approach a corner, fold the cording around the corner and continue whipstitching it in place. The cording will make for a slightly rounded corner. You may need to trim some of the excess backing fabric diagonally across the corner to make it easier to fold over the cording.

8. When all edges have been covered with yarn, it's time to add the twill tape. By hand, sew one edge of the twill tape as close to the whipped edges as possible with quilting thread that matches the color of your twill tape. Make sure to pleat the corners to allow enough tape to miter them when you sew the opposite edge.

Smooth Corners

To make a smooth edge, you'll need to stitch in each hole in the backing fabric so that the entire corded edge is covered and the backing fabric doesn't show through. When you come to a corner, however, stitching once in each hole may not be enough for adequate coverage. Try doubling up and taking two whipstitches per hole as you turn the corners. You'll end up with a nice rounded corner that is covered completely.

9. Make sure that the backing fabric does not extend beyond the unsewn edge of the twill tape. If it does, trim as necessary. Hand stitch the remaining edge of the twill tape in place, mitering the corners as you go.

Caring for Your Hooked Rug

Because they're made of wool, you'll find your hooked rugs to be quite durable and resilient. Do not wash or dry-clean them. To maintain their beauty and their life, periodically shake out the dust and sweep them with an electric broom or hand-held sweeper; never use a vacuum cleaner with beater bars on your rug!

If a spill occurs, dab it up with a damp cloth. Most spills will bead up on the wool, giving you time to blot them. If necessary, dampen a sponge or cloth and use a gentle soap sparingly to wipe away the spill. And just as it does for penny rugs, a masking tape lint roller does wonders on hooked rugs when it comes to removing pet hair.

Heart Duet

by Janet Carija Brandt

Janet Brandt is well known for her excellent use of color, favoring bright clear colors as opposed to the darker, overdyed wools used in more rustic-style projects. This pair of heart designs is stylish and sophisticated.

Heart Octet Penny Rug

This cheerful little penny rug features brightly colored wools and embroidery stitches. It is quilted with embroidery floss for added detail and dimension, and is finished with traditional quilt binding.

Finished size: 16¼" x 16¼"

Materials

Wool yardage amounts are based on 60"-wide wool. Wash new wool before using.

½ yard of solid yellow wool for background

½ yard of solid red wool for appliqués

1 fat quarter of cotton for rug backing

1 fat quarter of solid green cotton for rug binding

1 skein of yellow embroidery floss

1 skein of blue embroidery floss

Freezer paper

Black fine-point permanent marker

Optional: temporary spray adhesive

Cutting

Patterns for the appliqué shapes are on page 27. Make a freezer-paper template for each shape, referring to page 10 for directions.

From the yellow wool, cut:
- ◆ 1 square, 16¼" x 16¼"

From the red wool, cut:
- ◆ 8 hearts
- ◆ 20 tongues
- ◆ 4 corner tongues

From the green cotton, cut:
- ◆ 2 strips, 2½" x 42"

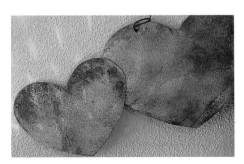

Making the Penny Rug

1. Fold the yellow background fabric into quarters and mark the center point with a pin. Use the photograph on page 25 as a placement guide. Line up the straight edges of the tongues with the straight edges of the background fabric and baste them in place. Position the hearts so that four of them point toward the center of the rug, leaving about ¼" between the hearts. The final four hearts fill in the corner spaces of the penny rug.

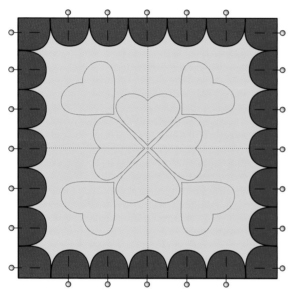

Pin or baste tongues in place.

Quick Basting with Spray Adhesive

Temporary spray adhesive allows you to place and reposition your appliqué shapes easily. Once you're satisfied with their placement, you can sew pin free. Simply follow the instructions on the can to spray the backs of the hearts and tongues, and arrange them on the background fabric.
Note: *Be sure to check the can label for proper usage instructions.*

2. Using two strands of the yellow embroidery floss, blanket stitch each heart and tongue in place.

3. To mark the chain-stitched border on the yellow wool background fabric, trace the pattern, opposite, onto freezer paper. The pattern given is for one quarter of the design. Match up the design along the dashed lines to make a full-size pattern. Press the freezer paper onto the center of the background fabric to use as a stitching guide.

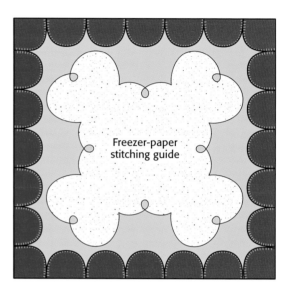

Freezer-paper stitching guide

4. Using two strands of the blue embroidery floss, chain stitch the decorative border around the hearts following the edge of the freezer-paper pattern. (See page 11 for the chain stitch and other embroidery stitches.) If desired, you can also chain stitch your name and date in one corner of the design.

5. Cover the back of the penny rug with the cotton backing fabric. Trim the edges of the backing fabric even with the wool square and baste the layers together with thread or pins.

6. Using two strands of blue embroidery floss, quilt around the center hearts and the outside of the tongue border, stitching about ¼" away from the design details.

7. Bind the penny rug as you would a quilt, using the 2½"-wide green cotton strips.

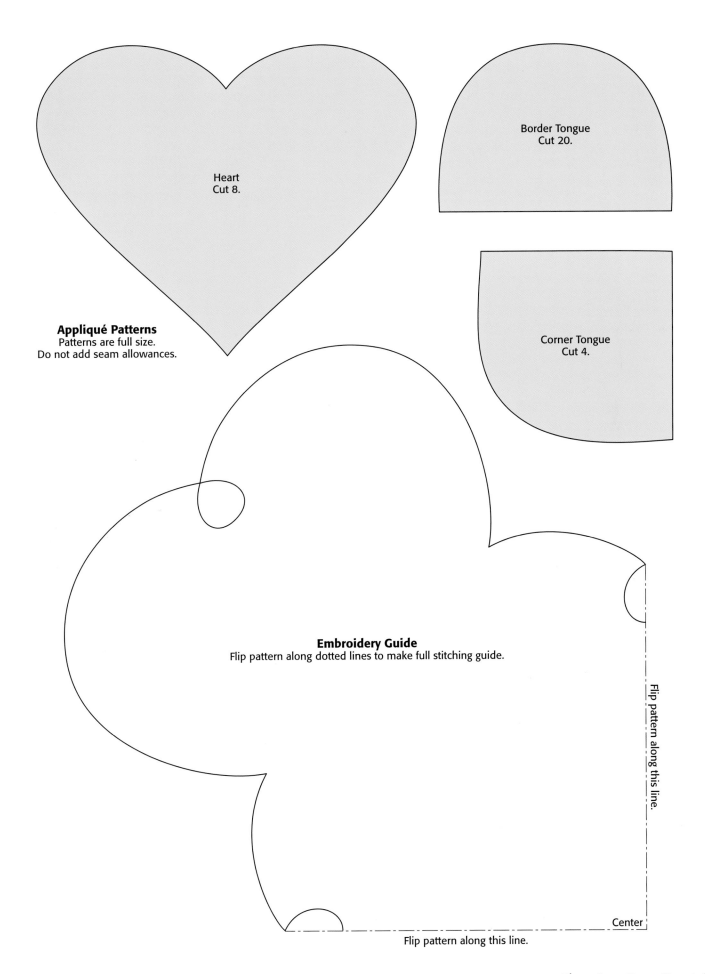

Heart
Cut 8.

Border Tongue
Cut 20.

Corner Tongue
Cut 4.

Appliqué Patterns
Patterns are full size.
Do not add seam allowances.

Embroidery Guide
Flip pattern along dotted lines to make full stitching guide.

Flip pattern along this line.

Flip pattern along this line.

Center

Heart Quartet Hooked Rug

Unlike most of the other hooked rugs in this book, Heart Quartet is hooked with narrow (⅛"-wide) strips, which allowed Janet to achieve fine details, such as the blue tendrils and gold dots in the tongues.

Finished size: 10" x 10"

Materials

Wool yardage amounts are based on 60"-wide wool. Wash new wool before using. Amounts allow for four times the area that will be hooked.

⅓ yard of solid yellow wool for background

⅓ yard of solid red wool for hearts and border

¼ yard of solid blue wool for scrollwork, hearts, and border

¼ yard of solid green wool for diamonds and border

¼ yard of solid gold wool for flowers

18" square of backing fabric (linen, monk's cloth, or Scottish burlap)

Red Dot Tracer or craft netting

Black permanent marker

Hooking the Rug

1. Enlarge the Heart Quartet pattern (page 31) 135%, and then transfer it onto your backing fabric using a permanent marker. See page 14 for details on transferring patterns.

2. Cut the wool into size 4 strips (⅛" wide) by using a strip cutter or your rotary cutter.

3. Using the photograph above as a guide, hook the rug design. Hook the outlines first, and then fill in the various areas with color.

Finishing the Rug

1. Block the rug. Lay it on a flat surface, such as your ironing board, cover it with a wet towel, and press the towel with the iron to steam the rug. If the rug is at all out of square, gently pull the rug to get it back into shape and allow the damp rug to dry overnight.

2. Bind the rug. For this project, Janet turned the excess rug backing fabric to the wrong side of the rug and folded the fabric at the corners to form miters. She hand stitched the miters in place with matching thread. With this finishing method, you do not need binding tape, wool, or yarn to finish the edges. For other ways to finish your rug, see "Finishing Details" on page 18.

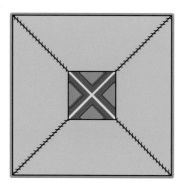

Fold rug backing fabric toward back of rug and whipstitch miters in place.

3. Sign and date your rug. You may want to sign your name on the back side with an indelible pen, attach a fabric label, or embroider your initials and the date on the front of the rug as Janet did.

Heart Quartet Hooked Rug Pattern
One square = ¼".
Enlarge pattern 135% to 10" x 10".

Snow Folks

by Tara Lynn Darr
of Sew Unique Creations

Tara has created a charming snow family in her penny rug, while featuring a solo guy in her coordinating hooked rug. Notice how the warm plaid wools make perfect scarves for these folks, whether they're appliquéd or hooked. The mottled blue fabrics in the backgrounds are reminiscent of a cold winter sky. You can practically feel the chill in the air!

Snow in Love
Penny Rug

This handsome snow family is quite dapper with plaid scarves, Mom's cap, and Dad's tall top hat. Designer Tara Lynn Darr used a combination of stitches, including blanket stitch, cross stitch, running stitch, and stars to give this piece lots of texture and whimsical appeal.

Finished size: 15½" x 13¾"

Materials

Wool yardage amounts are based on 60"-wide wool. Wash new wool before using.

½ yard of light blue wool for background and large pennies

9" x 12" piece of blue plaid wool for small pennies

9" x 12" piece of navy blue wool for small pennies

9" x 12" piece of cream wool for snowmen

5" x 7" piece of green wool for tree

4" x 4" piece each of 3 different plaids for scarves and cap

4" x 4" piece of black wool for top hat

2 skeins of cream embroidery floss

1 skein each of red, gold, orange, and black embroidery floss

#20 or #22 chenille needle or a medium-eye embroidery needle

Freezer paper

Black fine-point permanent marker

Tracing paper

10" x 10" piece of netting or tulle

Black chalk pencil (dressmaker's chalk)

Optional: glue stick

Cutting

Patterns for the appliqué shapes are on page 37. After enlarging the patterns, make a freezer-paper template for each shape, referring to page 10 for directions.

From the light blue wool, cut:
- 2 background ovals
- 44 large pennies

From the blue plaid wool, cut:
- 11 small pennies

From the navy blue wool, cut:
- 11 small pennies

From the cream wool, cut:
- 1 each of the snowmen

From the green wool, cut:
- 1 tree

From the three assorted plaid wools, cut:
- 1 each of the scarves and lady's cap

From the black wool, cut:
- 1 top hat
- 3 buttons

Making the Penny Rug

1. Using the appliqué placement guide opposite and referring to the project photograph on page 35, position the appliqué pieces onto one of the light blue ovals, overlapping them as indicated by the dashed lines on the placement guide. (Set aside the other oval and the large and small pennies for now.)

2. Once you are satisfied with the arrangement, daub a small amount of glue on the back of each piece to hold it in place for stitching, or pin the shapes in place.

3. Using two strands of embroidery floss, stitch the pieces in place. Follow the numerical order of the pattern pieces. The snowmen are stitched using black floss and a blanket stitch. The scarves, hats, and tree are stitched with a primitive stitch as shown below. Tara used black floss for the tree, red floss for the plaid hat and one scarf, cream floss for the top hat and buttons, and gold floss for the remaining scarf.
   Note: The bottom edge of the snowmen should be aligned with the bottom edge of the blue oval. Do not stitch them in place at this time.

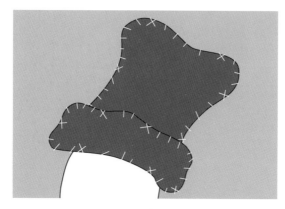

Primitive Appliqué Stitch
Take long whipstitch. Occasionally cross stitches over one another, if desired.

4. Trace the lettering "Snow in Love!" and the face details onto a piece of tracing paper. Place nylon netting or tulle over the traced lettering and use the black permanent marker to retrace the lettering onto the netting. Then place the netting over the area of the penny rug where the wording is to be stitched and retrace the letters onto the wool, this time using the black chalk pencil.

5. Remove the netting and, using two strands of cream floss, stitch the words with a short outline stitch. (See page 11 for stitch details.)

6. Place the netting over the snowmen and trace the facial details onto each snowman with the black chalk pencil.

7. Remove the netting and stitch the details as follows: Stitch each face using two strands of black floss. Stitch the noses with two strands of orange floss. Using two strands of black floss, stitch three Xs for buttons on the front of the large snowman on the left.

8. Once all the pieces are appliquéd and the stitching details have been added, layer the penny rug on top of the remaining light blue oval, aligning all edges. Pin or glue baste the layers together. Using two strands of cream floss, blanket stitch around the perimeter of the rug to hold the two layers together.

9. To make the pennies, use two strands of cream floss and blanket stitch each small navy blue and blue plaid penny to a large light blue penny. On the navy blue pennies, add a snowflake, as shown.

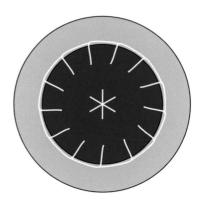

10. Layer each prepared penny on top of a plain light blue penny. Stitch around the perimeter of each using two strands of cream floss and the blanket stitch.

11. Arrange the completed pennies around the perimeter of the rug, alternating the navy blue and blue plaid pennies. Using cream floss, tack the pennies to the outer edge of the rug. When all pennies are attached, go back and tack them to one another where they abut, using a couple of small whipstitches.

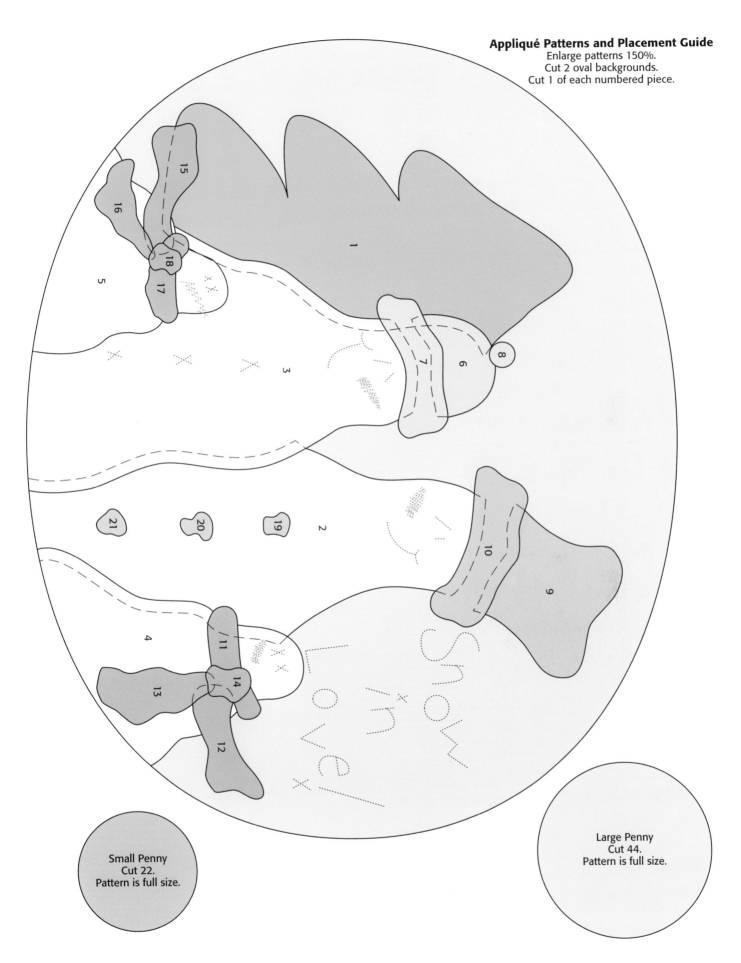

Appliqué Patterns and Placement Guide
Enlarge patterns 150%.
Cut 2 oval backgrounds.
Cut 1 of each numbered piece.

Small Penny
Cut 22.
Pattern is full size.

Large Penny
Cut 44.
Pattern is full size.

Just Another Flake Hooked Rug

*What a jolly little fellow! This snowman is guaranteed
not to melt, so he can adorn your home all winter long.*

Finished size: 10" x 10"

Materials

Wool yardage amounts are based on 60"-wide wool. Wash new wool before using. Amounts allow for four times the area that will be hooked.

16" x 24" piece of dusty blue wool for background

16" x 18" piece of plaid wool for scarf and inner border

12" x 16" piece of cream wool for snowman and snowflakes

4" x 16" piece of rust red wool for scarf

1" x 16" piece of pumpkin wool for nose

1" x 16" piece of dark brown wool for eyes

24" square of backing fabric (linen, monk's cloth, or Scottish burlap)

Red Dot Tracer or craft netting

Black permanent marker

Optional:

2 yards of 1"- or 2"-wide twill binding tape and hand quilting thread to match

2 yards of ⅜"-diameter cotton cording

25 yards of wool yarn for finishing edges

Hooking the Rug

1. Using a permanent marker, draw an 8½" square centered on the backing fabric. Draw another square ¾" outside the first square to mark the border area. This square should measure 10" x 10".

2. Trace the Just Another Flake pattern on page 41 onto your backing fabric, centering the design within the 8½" square. See page 14 for details on transferring patterns.

3. Cut the wool into size 6 strips (³⁄₁₆" wide) using a strip cutter or your rotary cutter.

4. Hook the rug in the following order:

- Outline the scarf in plaid wool. Fill in the scarf using the rust red wool.

- Hook the nose with pumpkin wool.

- Hook the eyes with dark brown wool.
  Note: For the finer lines of the eyes, you can trim the dark brown wool strips to a scant 1/16" wide.

- Outline the snowman with cream wool and then fill in the body using wool of the same color. Hook the snowflakes also in cream wool.

- Using dusty blue wool, hook two rows around the inside perimeter of the 8½" square, hooking just inside the drawn lines. Then hook one or two rows of dusty blue wool around the snowman before filling in the rest of the background.

- Hook the outer border using plaid wool. Hook just inside the marked outline first, and then fill in the remaining rows.

Hooking Backgrounds

Add character and eye appeal to your project by hooking the background areas in circles or wavy lines rather than in straight rows. Doing so will add movement to the hooked piece and make the snowflakes appear to be drifting in the air.

Finishing the Rug

This rug is finished by whipping wool yarn over cotton cording and the edge of the rug. For complete details on this type of edge finish, please see "Finishing Details" on page 18. You'll also find instructions for other options for finishing your rug. If you choose to use the twill tape and cotton cording called for in this method, be sure to preshrink each of them by soaking them in warm water and allowing them to air-dry before using.

1. Block the rug. Lay it on a flat surface, such as your ironing board, cover it with a wet towel, and press the towel with the iron to steam the rug. If the rug is at all out of square, gently pull it back into shape and allow the damp rug to dry overnight.

2. Bind the rug using your preferred method.

3. Sign and date your rug. You may sign your name on the binding tape on the back of the rug with an indelible pen, or, if you haven't used binding tape, you can make a fabric label and hand stitch it to the back of your rug.

**Just Another Flake
Hooked Rug Pattern**
Pattern is full size.

Horses

by Tonee White

Houses, pets, barnyard animals, and flowers were all part of daily farm and prairie life and thus appeared as common themes in antique rugs. The horses in designer Tonee White's rugs are similar to those used in other Early American artistic endeavors, such as weather vanes and wood carvings.

Horse
Penny Rug

Twenty little horseshoes, each "nailed" to wool tongues with French knots,
make a clever finishing touch to this dapper penny rug. If horseshoes
indeed symbolize good luck, this rug must be full of good fortune!

Finished size: 26" x 18"

Materials

Wool yardage amounts are based on 60"-wide wool. Wash new wool before using.

¾ yard of medium blue wool for background and backing

½ yard of mottled light blue wool for center oval

¼ yard of dark gold wool for horse and horseshoes

¼ yard of off-white wool for stars and tongues

⅛ yard or scrap of pink wool for stripes

Gold, pink, and dark brown floss or top-stitching thread

Freezer paper

Black permanent fine-point marker

Cutting

Patterns for the appliqué shapes are on pages 46–49. After enlarging the patterns, make a freezer-paper template for each shape, referring to page 10 for directions.

From the medium blue wool, cut:
- 2 of piece A for background and backing

From the mottled light blue wool, cut:
- 1 of oval B for rug center

From the dark gold wool, cut:
- 1 horse
- 20 horseshoes

From the off-white wool, cut:
- 5 stars
- 1 stripe F
- 20 tongues

From the pink wool, cut:
- 1 each of stripes C, D, and E

Making the Penny Rug

1. Position the pink and white stripes along the bottom edge of oval B. Place the longest pink stripe (C) approximately ⅜" from the bottom edge. Refer to the photograph on page 45 for placement. Position the horse above the stripes and then arch the five stars above the horse. Pin all motifs in place.

2. Using gold top-stitching thread or two strands of embroidery floss, appliqué the horse and pink stripes in place using a blanket stitch.

3. Using pink top-stitching thread or floss, appliqué the stars and white stripe in place, as in step 2.

4. Center the appliquéd oval on top of one of the scalloped medium blue background pieces (A) and pin in place. Blanket stitch the oval to the background piece with gold thread or floss.

5. Referring to the project photograph, position a white tongue on each blue scallop. Blanket stitch in place with gold thread.

6. Center a horseshoe in each white tongue. Anchor them in place with French knots. In the project shown, the horseshoes have nine French knots each, stitched with two strands of dark brown floss or top-stitching thread.

7. Place the finished rug top on the remaining scalloped backing, matching all edges. Pin or baste the two layers together, and then blanket stitch around all outer edges with gold thread or floss.

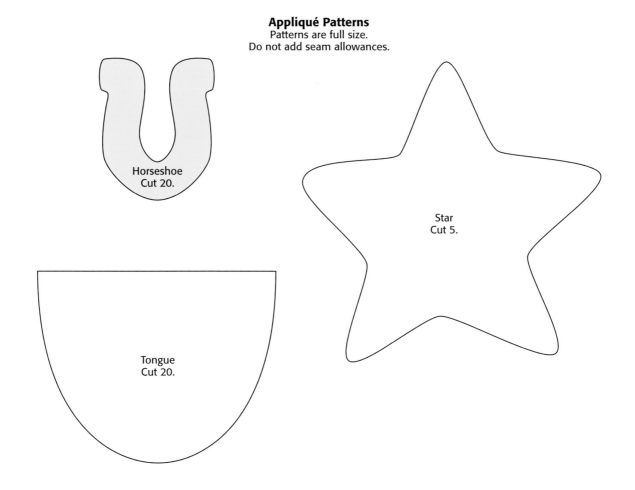

Appliqué Patterns
Patterns are full size.
Do not add seam allowances.

Horseshoe
Cut 20.

Star
Cut 5.

Tongue
Cut 20.

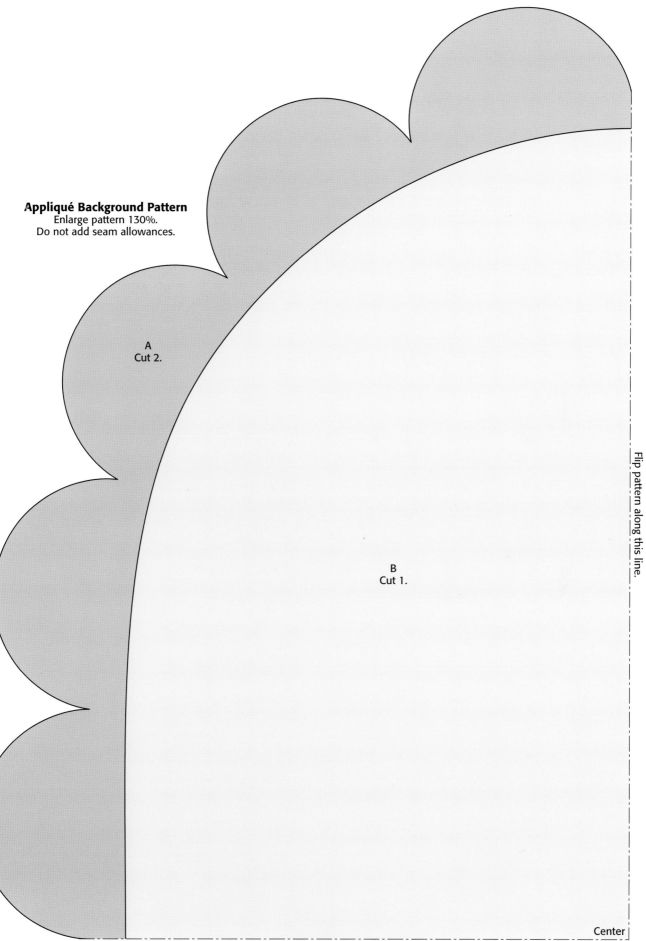

Appliqué Background Pattern
Enlarge pattern 130%.
Do not add seam allowances.

A
Cut 2.

B
Cut 1.

Flip pattern along this line.

Center

Flip pattern along this line.

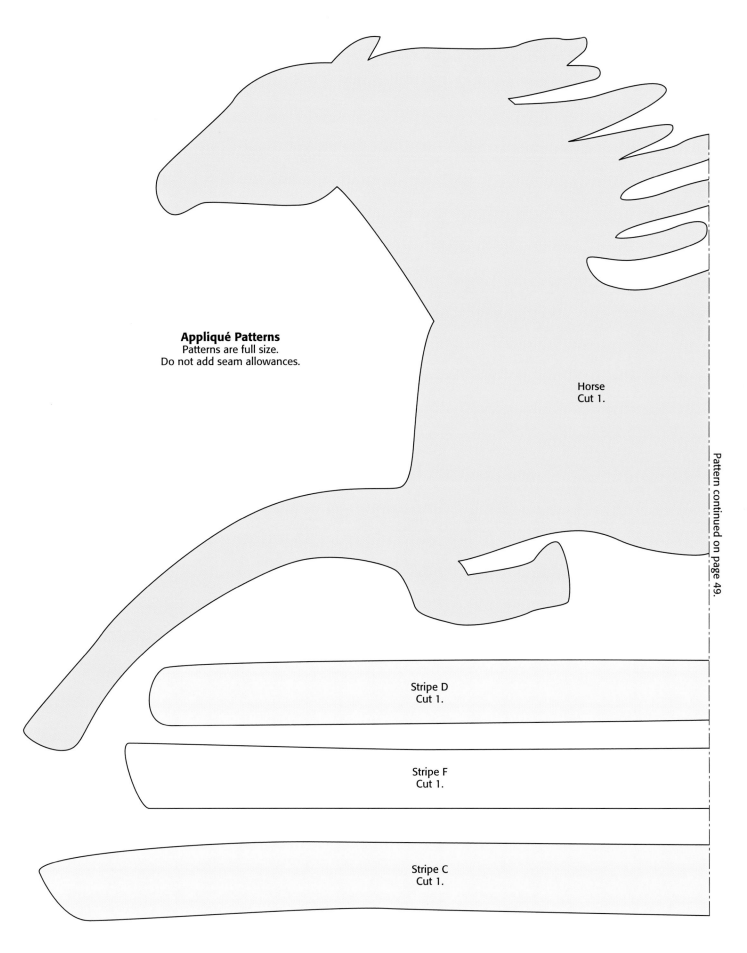

Appliqué Patterns
Patterns are full size.
Do not add seam allowances.

Horse
Cut 1.

Pattern continued on page 49.

Stripe D
Cut 1.

Stripe F
Cut 1.

Stripe C
Cut 1.

Appliqué Patterns
Patterns are full size.
Do not add seam allowances.

Pattern continued on page 48.

Stripe E
Cut 1.

Horse
Hooked Rug

The subtle coloration of stars and stripes, along with loops hooked in a swirling pattern, provides an interesting background to the main event in this rug—the running horse. Notice how the swirls give dimension to the large background areas, adding movement and excitement that straight lines of hooked loops couldn't provide. Thanks to Bev Conway for her help in color planning this rug.

Finished size: 32" x 24"

Materials

Wool yardage amounts are based on 60"-wide wool. Wash new wool before using. Amounts allow for four times the area that will be hooked.

⅝ yard total of assorted light mottled blue-gray wools for star background and horse

⅜ yard total of assorted light mottled peach wools for stars and stripes

¾ yard total of assorted deep teal wools for background

⅓ yard of light gold wool for background

⅛ yard of dark peach wool for stripes

Scrap of dark gold wool to outline stars

32" x 40" piece of backing fabric (linen, monk's cloth, or Scottish burlap)

Red Dot Tracer or craft netting

Black permanent marker

Optional: 3 ounces of teal blue bulky-weight yarn for binding

Hooking the Rug

1. Enlarge the Horse pattern (page 53) 340% and then transfer the design onto your backing fabric. See "Transferring Designs" on page 14 for more information.

2. Cut the wool into size 7 or size 8 strips (¼" wide) using a strip cutter or your rotary cutter. You may want to cut a few strips a bit narrower for smaller areas of the horse mane and tail, but you can do that by hand as the need arises.

3. Hook the rug in the following order:

   ◆ Hook the horse. Notice the direction in which Tonee hooked the loops to make the legs look as if they're moving.

   ◆ Using dark gold strips, outline the stars, and then fill them in with the light peach strips.

   ◆ Hook the background areas, referring to the photograph above for color placement.

Hooking in Circles

This rug has some large background areas, which could be boring to look at if hooked in straight, parallel lines. To make the background more interesting, Tonee hooked circles and swirls in the large blue areas. To do this, simply mark the designs you want to hook onto the backing fabric. Hook the swirled lines first and then fill in, hooking along your already hooked curves. You don't need to measure the circles, use templates, or even follow the lines exactly, as the markings will be covered by all the hooked loops.

Finishing the Rug

This rug was finished by whipping the edges with wool yarn. For complete details on this type of edge finish, please see "Finishing Details" on page 18. You'll also find instructions for other options for finishing your rug.

1. Block the rug. Lay it on a flat surface, such as your ironing board, cover it with a wet towel, and press the towel with the iron to steam the rug. If the rug is at all out of square, gently pull it back into shape and allow the damp rug to dry overnight.

2. Bind the rug using your preferred method.

3. Sign and date your rug. If you turn the backing fabric or rug tape to the back of the rug, you may sign your name on the edge of this fabric with an indelible pen, or you can make a fabric label and hand stitch it to the back of your rug.

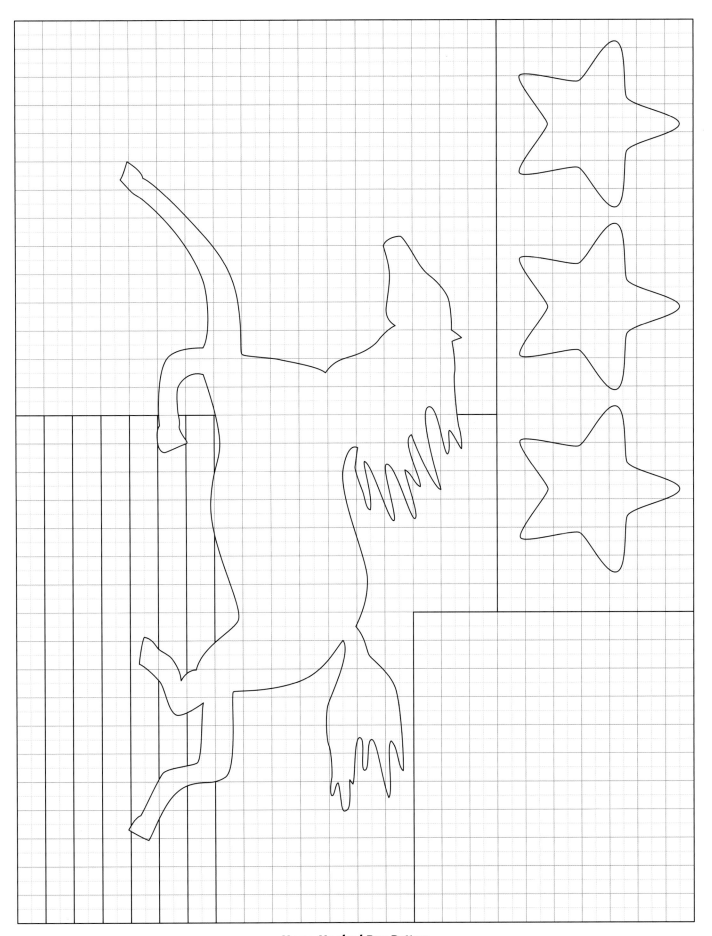

Horse Hooked Rug Pattern
One square = ½".
Enlarge 200% and then 170%
(340% total) to 26" x 18".

Sheep in the Meadow

by Whimsicals

As Jackie Conaway and Terri Degenkolb of Whimsicals were working on these projects, the old nursery rhyme Little Boy Blue kept running through their heads. They named these pieces for the sheep that played in the meadow.

Little Boy Blue, come blow your horn!
The sheep's in the meadow,
the cow's in the corn.
Where's the little boy who
looks after the sheep?
Under the haystack, fast asleep.

Sheep in the Meadow Penny Rug

Three little sheep are frolicking on this generously sized penny rug,
which is perfect to display on a round dining table.

Materials

*Wool yardage amounts are based on 60"-wide wool.
Wash new wool before using.*

⅞ yard of brown plaid wool for background and
tongues

⅞ yard of dark wool for rug backing

8" x 18" of dark red wool for berries and pennies

7" x 18" of off-white wool for sheep bodies

3" x 12" of tan wool for sheep ears and legs

3" x 12" of gold wool for stars

3" x 6" of beige wool for sheep heads

1" x 8" of green wool for vines

2 skeins of tan embroidery floss

2 skeins of dark brown or black embroidery floss

Freezer paper

Newspaper

Black fine-point permanent marker

Optional: glue stick or spray adhesive

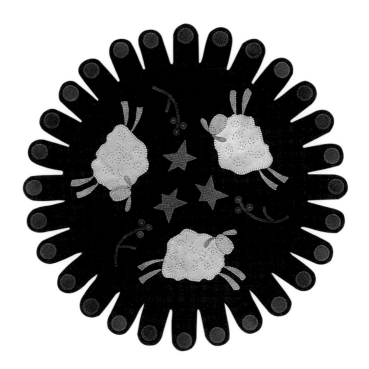

Finished size: 32" diameter, including tongues

Cutting

Patterns for the appliqué shapes are on pages 58–59.
Make a freezer-paper template for each shape, referring to page 14 for directions. For the background
circle, make a 24"-diameter circle pattern from
newspaper as instructed below right.

From the brown plaid wool, cut:
- One 24"-diameter circle*
- 28 tongues

From the off-white wool, cut:
- 3 sheep bodies

From the beige wool, cut:
- 3 sheep heads

From the tan wool, cut:
- 3 sets of ears
- 3 sets of legs

From the gold wool, cut:
- 3 stars

From the dark red wool, cut:
- 9 berries
- 28 pennies

From the green wool, cut:
- 3 strips, ¼" x 6"
- 3 strips, ¼" x 2"

From the dark wool for backing, cut:
- One 24"-diameter circle*

** On a large sheet of newspaper, mark the center point
and then measure 12" from the center point as a guide.
Tie one end of a piece of string around a pencil. Place
the pencil point on the 12" mark. Pull the string taut,
hold the end in place at the center mark, and use the
string compass to mark the circle. Cut out the circle and
pin the pattern onto the fabric.*

Making the Penny Rug

1. Position the appliqué pieces (except for the tongues and red pennies) on the 24" brown plaid circle, referring to the project photograph on page 57 for placement. Pin or glue baste in place.

2. Using two strands of tan embroidery floss for all appliqué, attach the pieces as follows:
   - Blanket stitch the sheep bodies, faces, and the stars to the background.
   - Stitch the legs and ears in place using a running stitch around their edges.
   - Attach the vines with running stitches through the center of the vines.
   - Stitch the berries in place with a double cross-stitch in the center of each.

3. Add embroidery details to the sheep with the tan floss. Stitch the sheep's eyes with one long straight stitch for each eye. Use long running stitches to add the curlicues to the sheep's bodies.

4. Position a red penny on the curved end of each brown plaid tongue and blanket stitch in place with two strands of tan embroidery floss.

5. Blanket stitch around the long sides and curved ends of the tongues, using two strands of dark brown or black floss. There is no need to stitch the short straight ends, as they will not be seen.

6. Place the penny rug on top of the 24" dark wool backing circle, wrong sides together. Position the tongues around the perimeter of the penny rug, tucking them in between the rug and backing layers. Approximately ½" of the tongue should be sandwiched between the layers. Pin them in place.

7. Using two strands of dark brown or black floss, blanket stitch around the edge of the rug, securing the pennies and the backing in place.

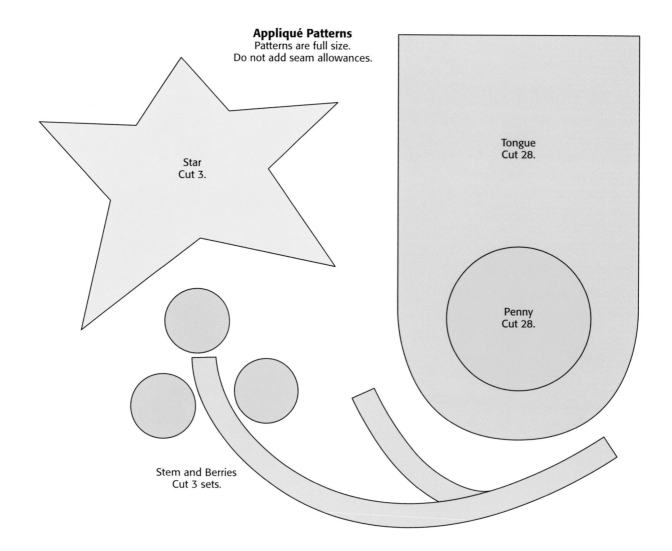

Appliqué Patterns
Patterns are full size.
Do not add seam allowances.

Star
Cut 3.

Tongue
Cut 28.

Penny
Cut 28.

Stem and Berries
Cut 3 sets.

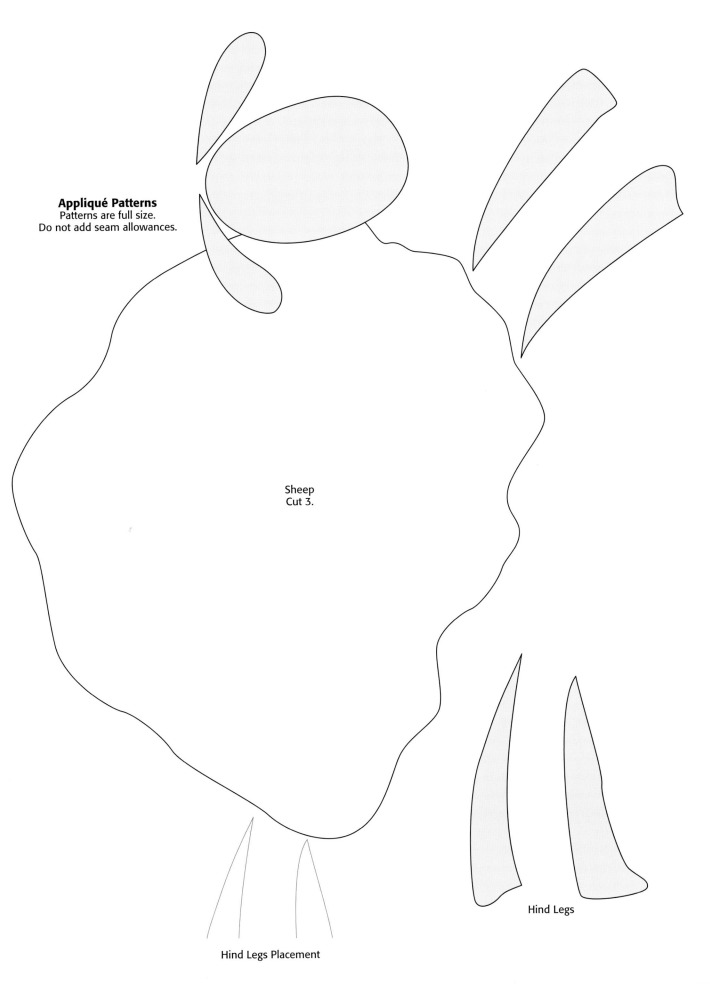

Appliqué Patterns
Patterns are full size.
Do not add seam allowances.

Sheep
Cut 3.

Hind Legs

Hind Legs Placement

Sheep in the Meadow Hooked Rug

Many shades of assorted brown fabrics add interest to the rug background, while the sheep gets his woolly look from swirls hooked in tan and the remainder of the body hooked in a stipple style. That's where individual loops are hooked in random directions, rather than in a straight line. No wonder this little fellow is jumping for joy!

Finished size: 18" x 14"

Materials

Wool yardage amounts are based on 60"-wide wool. Wash new wool before using. Amounts allow for four times the area that will be hooked.

4 fat quarters of assorted brown wools for background

1 fat eighth of off-white wool for sheep body

1 fat eighth of gold wool for stars

4" x 18" of beige wool for head

4" x 18" of tan wool for ears, legs, and swirls

4" x 18" of green wool for vines

3" x 18" of red wool for berries

Scrap of black wool for eyes

22" x 26" of backing fabric (linen, monk's cloth, or Scottish burlap)

Red Dot Tracer or craft netting

Black permanent marker

Hooking the Rug

1. Draw a 14" x 18" rectangle centered on your backing fabric. Referring to the project photograph above and using the sheep, star, and berry patterns on pages 58 and 59, draw the rug design onto the Red Dot Tracer paper, and then transfer the pattern onto your backing fabric, centering the design within the 14" x 18" rectangle. See page 14 for details on transferring patterns.

   Alternately, you can enlarge the hooked rug pattern (page 63) 200% and transfer it to the backing fabric.

2. Cut the wool into size 8 strips (¼" wide) using a strip cutter or your rotary cutter.

3. Using the photograph as a guide, hook the rug design in the following order:

- Hook the swirls in the sheep with tan wool, and then hook the remainder of the sheep's body with off-white wool.

- Hook the sheep's eyes in black and then hook the head in beige wool.

- Hook the ears and legs in tan wool.

- Hook the stars in gold, the vines in green, and the berries in red.

- Fill in the background with the assorted brown wools, randomly mixing up the colors as you go, to create an antique look.

Finishing the Rug

This rug is finished by whipping wool yarn over jute cording and the edge of the rug. For complete details on this type of edge finish, please see "Finishing Details" on page 18. You'll also find instructions for other options for finishing your rug.

1. Block the rug. Lay it on a flat surface, such as your ironing board, cover it with a wet towel, and press the towel with the iron to steam the rug. If the rug is at all out of square, gently pull it back into shape and allow the damp rug to dry overnight.

2. Bind the rug using your desired method.

3. Sign and date your rug. If you haven't used binding tape, you can make a fabric label and hand stitch it to the back of your rug.

Sheep Hooked Rug Pattern
One square = ½".
Enlarge pattern 200% to 14" x 18".

Betsy's Best

by Little Quilts

This patriotic duo from Little Quilts combines folk art flower motifs with the ever-popular stars and stripes. Notice how the use of old gold and cranberry reds give these projects an aged quality that will help them fit right in with a display of your favorite antiques or collectibles.

Flag Penny Rug

This penny rug combines traditional quilt piecing with blanket-stitch appliqué. Old gold thread accents the appliqué shapes as well as creates waves of quilting in the white stripes of the flag.

Finished size: 21½" x 10½"

Materials

Wool yardage amounts are based on 60"-wide wool. Wash new wool before using.

¼ yard of cranberry wool for stripes

¼ yard of white wool for stripes

⅛ yard of navy wool for star field and tongues

3" x 15" piece of gold wool for star, flower center, and borders

6" x 6" piece of green wool for leaves

4" x 4" piece of red wool for flower

1 skein of old gold wool floss

1 fat quarter of cotton backing fabric

Freezer paper

Black fine-point permanent marker

Optional: fusible web

Cutting

Patterns for the appliqué shapes are on page 69. Make a freezer-paper template for the tongues, referring to page 10 for directions. Little Quilts fused the other appliqué shapes in place before stitching. To do so, trace the appliqué patterns onto the paper-backing side of fusible web for your templates.

The dimensions for the stripes are given below, but we recommend that you tear rather than cut the stripes. Tearing is more accurate than rotary cutting when it comes to keeping the grain on line. Tear the strips so they are 1⅜" wide and a bit longer than the size listed below. They can be trimmed to the correct length after the sewing and pressing is complete.

From the cranberry wool, tear:
- 3 strips, 1⅜" x 9½"
- 4 strips, 1⅜" x 16"

From the white wool, tear:
- 3 strips, 1⅜" x 9½"
- 3 strips, 1⅜" x 16"

From the navy wool, cut:
- 1 rectangle, 5¾" x 6¾"
- 12 tongues

From the gold wool, tear:
- 2 strips, 1½" x 11⅜"

From the remaining gold wool, cut:
- 1 star
- 1 flower center

From the green wool, cut
- 3 leaves

From the red wool, cut:
- 1 flower

Making the Penny Rug

Set the stitch length on your sewing machine to a little longer than normal. This will help the seam to relax when pressed.

1. Using a ¼" seam allowance, sew the three short cranberry and three short white strips together, alternating the colors. Press the seams open. Trim this section to 9¼" long.

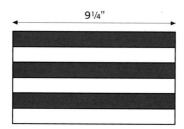

2. Sew four long cranberry and three long white strips together, alternating the colors. Press the seams open. Trim this section to 15½" long.

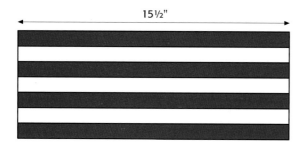

3. Sew the navy rectangle to the short striped unit so that when the navy wool is on the left, a cranberry strip is at the top of the unit. Press the seam toward the navy rectangle.

4. Sew the top and bottom units together to form a flag. Press the seam open. If necessary, trim the completed flag so that it measures 11⅜" x 15½". If you need to trim, trim evenly from both the top and bottom of the flag so that you don't have an exceptionally narrow red strip at either the top or bottom.

5. Sew a gold strip on each short end of the flag, trimming the length to fit if necessary. Press the seams toward the gold strips.

6. Place the flower, star, and leaves on the blue star field. Pin or fuse in place. Blanket stitch around each shape using one strand of gold wool floss.

7. Blanket stitch around each tongue using one strand of gold wool floss.

8. Turn under ¼" along each edge of the flag and baste in place. Place six tongues along each end of the rug and pin or baste them in place.

9. From the backing fabric, cut a rectangle 11⅞" x 16". Press under the edges of the cotton backing fabric ¼" or as needed to fit the back of the flag. Pin the backing to the flag, wrong sides together.

10. Blanket stitch around the perimeter of the flag with one strand of gold wool floss, stitching through all layers to secure the tongues and backing.

11. Again using one strand of gold wool floss and a long running stitch, quilt a wavy line on each white stripe, stitching through all layers.

Appliqué Patterns
Patterns are full size.
Do not add seam allowances.

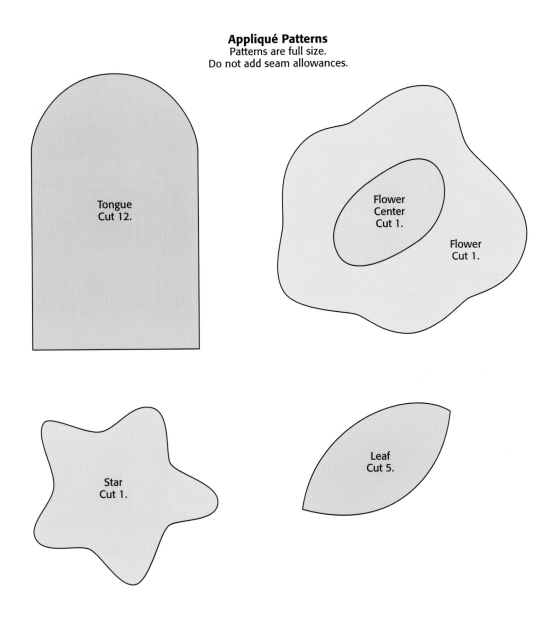

Tongue
Cut 12.

Flower
Center
Cut 1.

Flower
Cut 1.

Star
Cut 1.

Leaf
Cut 5.

Flag
Hooked Rug

*Plaid and checked wools give this hooked mat plenty of
visual texture, making it a perfect Americana centerpiece
for your table or to display on the wall.*

Finished size: 14½" x 10¼"

Materials

Wool yardage amounts are based on 60"-wide wool. Wash new wool before using. Amounts allow for four times the area that will be hooked.

¼ yard of red wool for stripes

¼ yard of tan-and-white check wool for stripes

⅛ yard of blue wool for star field

⅛ yard of red plaid or tweed wool for flowers and border

⅛ yard of gold wool for stars and flower centers

Scraps of light gold wool for flower centers

Scraps of assorted green wools for leaves and stems

18" x 22" of backing fabric (linen, monk's cloth, or Scottish burlap)

Red Dot Tracer or craft netting

Black permanent marker

1¾ yards of twill rug binding tape

Hooking the Rug

1. Enlarge the flag pattern (page 73) 150% and then transfer the design onto your rug backing fabric, referring to page 14 for details on transferring patterns.

2. If you want to finish your rug with twill binding tape, we suggest you sew the tape onto the rug backing fabric first, referring to page 18 for details.

3. Cut the wool into size 8 strips (¼" wide) by using a strip cutter or your rotary cutter.

4. Using the photograph as a guide, hook the design in the following order:

   ◆ Hook the flowers in red plaid wool.

   ◆ Outline the flower centers in light gold and then fill in with gold wool.

   ◆ Hook the stars in gold wool.

   ◆ Hook the leaves and stems in the green wools.

   ◆ Hook one row of red plaid loops around the perimeter of the rug, close to the binding tape.

   ◆ Hook the stripes and the star field. Little Quilts hooked these elements in straight parallel rows to accentuate the flag stripes.

Finishing the Rug

This rug is finished with twill rug binding tape, which is sewn to the edges of the backing fabric before hooking. For complete details on this type of edge finish, please see "Finishing Details" on page 18. You'll also find instructions for other options for finishing your rug.

1. Block the rug. Lay it on a flat surface, such as your ironing board, cover it with a wet towel, and press the towel with the iron to steam the rug. If the rug is at all out of square, gently pull it back into shape and allow the damp rug to dry overnight.

2. Sew the binding tape to the back of the rug with a whipstitch, mitering the corners.

3. Sign and date your rug. If you've used binding tape, you can write or embroider the information on the tape, or you can make a fabric label and hand stitch it to the back of your rug.

Flag Hooked Rug Pattern
One square = ¼".
Enlarge pattern 150% to 10¼" x 14½".

Bird and Flower

by Kindred Spirits

When Kindred Spirits went to the fabric shop looking for a "to-die-for" piece of tapestry, they were captivated by this linen crewelwork with leaves and flowers stitched in wool. They created the hooking and appliqué designs to match the tapestry. We suggest you try the same thing. You can make the pillow and bag as directed, but you may want to alter your motifs and colors to coordinate with a favorite tapestry fabric.

Bird and Flower Appliquéd Bag

For a one-of-a-kind bag, select a tapestry or home-decorating fabric that you love, and then plan your appliqué color scheme around that fabric. For this bag, the artists used the blue, green, camel, and wine colors from the pretty floral crewelwork, but your bird and blossoms could be any color that suits you.

Materials

Wool yardage amounts are based on 60"-wide wool. Wash new wool before using.

½ yard of tapestry fabric for top front and back of bag

¼ yard of plaid wool for side and bottom panels of bag and tab closure

10" x 16" piece of blue wool for appliqué panel on front of bag, strap holders, and appliqué details

3" x 12" scrap of burgundy wool for wing, flower, and tongue appliqués

3" x 12" scrap of tan plaid wool for flower and tongue appliqués

3" x 9" scrap of tan check wool for bird appliqué

3" x 6" scrap of green wool for leaves and stems appliqué and covered button

⅝ yard of wool for bag lining

Embroidery floss to match or contrast (Khaki and medium brown were used here.)

Two ½"-wide lengths of leather strapping for handles (Those shown are 36"-long; if you want shorter handles, determine how long you want them to be and add 3" per strap.)

2"-diameter covered button

Freezer paper

Black permanent fine-point marker

Cutting

Patterns for the appliqué shapes are on pages 80–81. Make a freezer-paper template for each shape, referring to page 10 for directions.

From the burgundy wool, cut:
- 1 wing
- 2 flower tops
- 4 medium tongues

From the tan check wool, cut:
- 1 bird

From the blue wool, cut:
- 1 strip, 1½" x 16"
- 1 rectangle, 8" x 14"
- 4 small tongues
- 2 zigzag strips for flowers

Finished size: 13" x 16½" x 2½"

From the scrap of tan plaid wool, cut:
- 2 flowers
- 4 large tongues
- 1 beak

From the scrap of green wool, cut:
- 2 stems
- 2 leaves
- One 3"-diameter circle for button cover (or size specified with your button directions)

From the tapestry fabric, cut:
- 1 bag back, 14" x 17½"
- 1 bag front, 10½" x 14"

From the plaid wool, cut:
- 2 strips, 3½" x 17½"
- 1 strip, 3½" x 14"
- 2 front closure tabs

From the lining fabric, cut:
- 2 rectangles, 14" x 17"
- 2 strips, 3½" x 17½"
- 1 strip, 3½" x 14"

Appliquéing the Bag

1. Stitch the layered appliqué shapes together before attaching them to the background fabric. Use either a blanket stitch or whipstitch and two strands of floss to sew the wing to the bird and the three layers of flowers together. Then stitch the small tongues to the medium tongues and stitch these units to the large tongues.

2. Place the layered shapes on the 8" x 14" background wool, referring to the project photograph on page 77 for placement. Be sure to allow for ½" seam allowances along all edges; do not appliqué anything too close to the edges. When you are satisfied with the placement, appliqué the tongues, stems, flowers, leaves, and bird in place.

3. Add embroidery stitches to embellish the appliqué. The bird has a starburst eye with a French knot in the center. The wing has three rows of feather stitches. The top edge of the flowers are textured with French knots stitched in each point, and the small tongues have a large cross-stitched X in the centers. In addition, use a chain or backstitch to add legs and feet to the bird so that he appears to be standing on the second tongue from the left. For more details on these embroidery stitches, see page 11.

Assembling the Bag

All seam allowances are ½" wide unless otherwise stated. Seams are sewn with right sides together. Press the seams open or to one side, whichever seems less bulky, depending on your fabric.

1. Sew the appliqué panel to the bottom of the 10½" x 14" tapestry fabric to make the front of the bag.

2. Sew the bag bottom panel between the two side panels.

3. Sew the bag front and back to the side-bottom panels, matching the raw edges at the top of the bag and the side-bottom seams to the bottom corners of the bag. Pivot at the corners.

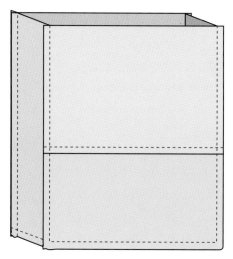

Sew the side and bottom panel strip to the front and back of the bag, pivoting at the corners.

4. Sew the lining pieces together in the same fashion. However, on one of the long side seams, leave a 6"- to 8"-long opening for turning the bag right side out.

5. Prepare the four wool strips that will hold the leather straps in place. Fold the 1½" x 16" strip lengthwise into thirds. Stitch along each folded edge to secure. Cut the long strip into four 4"-long segments.

4"

6. Prepare the tab closure. Sew the two tab pieces right sides together with a ¼" seam allowance, leaving the top straight edge open. Trim the seam and clip the corners, and then turn the tab right side out. Press.

7. To assemble the bag, place the lining and the bag right sides together with the side seams matching and the top raw edges aligned. Center the button tab along the back edge of the bag. Slip it in place between the bag back and lining, with raw edges even. Pin it in place. Likewise, place the four strips that will hold the leather straps. Fold each 4" strip in half and pin one in place 3" from each

side seam so you have two loops on the bag front and two on the bag back. The folded edges should be between the bag and the lining layers; the raw ends of the loops should be even with the raw edges of the bag and lining.

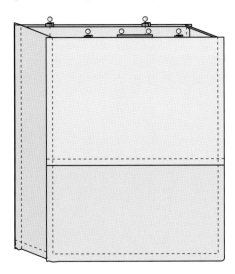

8. Stitch all the way around the top of the bag using a ½" seam. Stitch over each loop several times to reinforce it.

9. Turn the bag right side out, through the opening in the lining. Press. Either slipstitch the lining opening closed or use a sewing machine for more durability.

10. Follow the instructions on the covered button package to make the button. It is easier to do any stitching on the covered button if you place a small amount of stuffing or batting between the wool and the button. Stitch your initials or any desired design on the button.

11. Make a buttonhole on the tab to accommodate the button and sew the button in place on the bag.

12. Attach the leather straps. Put the ends of one strap through the loops on the front of the bag. Fold each end of the strap up about 1½" and paper clip in place. Make sure the straps are not twisted. Try on the bag for length and make any adjustments. When you are satisfied with the strap length, use a leather needle and strong thread (such as buttonhole twist or upholstery thread) and stitch through the layers of leather to hold them in place. Or take your bag to a shoe repair or saddle shop and ask them to stitch the leather in place by machine.

Buttonhole by Hand

It's difficult at best to make a 2" buttonhole on most home sewing machines. Since the rest of the bag shows off your hand embroidery, why not carry the look through to the buttonhole, too?

First, determine how long your buttonhole needs to be. Wrap a string, ribbon, or piece of floss around the center of the button and pin the ends together exactly where they meet. Slip the button out of the loop and flatten the string or ribbon. The distance from the pin to the fold is how long your buttonhole needs to be.

Next, mark the placement of a horizontal buttonhole on the tab with a chalk pencil, a marker, or pins. Cut from one end of the marking to the other to create the opening.

To secure the buttonhole edges, use a buttonhole stitch (or simple whipstitch as we did), all around the opening, using two strands of embroidery floss.

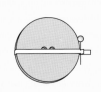

Wrap button to measure size for buttonhole.

Buttonhole or whipstitch around buttonhole.

An alternative is to simply use the large button as decoration and sew a large snap on the underside of the tab to use as the closure. This option will put less wear and tear on the tab and the button.

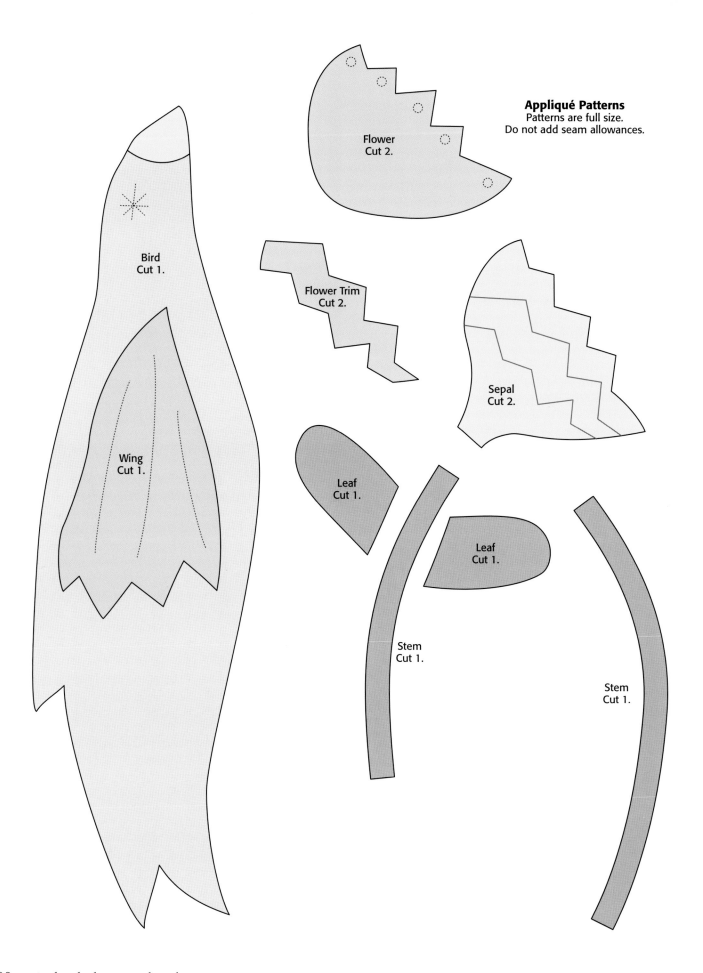

Appliqué Patterns
Patterns are full size.
Do not add seam allowances.

Flower
Cut 2.

Bird
Cut 1.

Flower Trim
Cut 2.

Sepal
Cut 2.

Wing
Cut 1.

Leaf
Cut 1.

Leaf
Cut 1.

Stem
Cut 1.

Stem
Cut 1.

Appliqué and Tab Closure Patterns

Patterns are full size.
Do not add seam allowances.

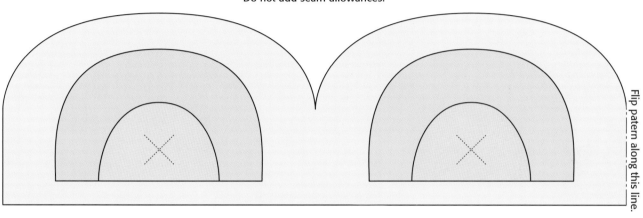

Flip pattern along this line.

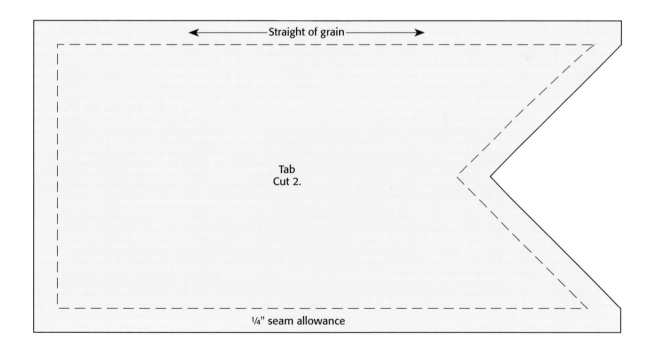

Straight of grain

Tab
Cut 2.

¼" seam allowance

Bird and Flower
Hooked Pillow

The pillow sleeve on this project is hooked to coordinate with the same linen crewelwork fabric used for the Bird and Flower bag. While the artists like to hook designs like this into wool, for this particular project they used a dark linen rug-backing fabric because it blended perfectly with the linen embroidered fabric. If you choose a tapestry fabric for your pillow, you may find that hooking the bird and flower into wool is the way to go!

Materials

Wool yardage amounts are based on 60"-wide wool. Amounts allow for four times the area that will be hooked. Wash new wool before using.

⅝ yard of tapestry fabric for pillow front and back*

22" x 42" piece of dark linen rug-hooking foundation fabric for the hooked sleeve

Wool for hooking:

    15" x 18" piece of gold wool for border

    15" x 15" piece of blue wool for border

    6" x 15" piece of red wool for flowers and bird

    5" x 15" piece of brown tweed for bird

    4" x 15" piece of green wool for stems and leaves

    1" x 15" piece of cream wool for the flower and bird's eye

Small strip of black wool for bird's eye

Embroidery floss

Four 1" or 1⅛" diameter buttons

Polyfil or other stuffing material

Red Dot Tracer or craft netting

Black permanent marker

  * *The pillow shown uses tapestry fabric on the pillow front and wool on the back. The yardage given is sufficient to make both the front and back, using the same fabric. However, if your tapestry fabric is quite expensive, you may want to buy a narrower piece of fabric (⅜ yard) and piece two segments together for the pillow front (the seam on the front will be hidden by the hooked sleeve when finished), and then use a coordinating piece of wool for the pillow back. We pieced the pillow back together from scraps too.*

Finished pillow size: 25" x 17½"

Finished sleeve, unbuttoned.

Hooking the Sleeve

1. Serge or zigzag the edges of the linen rug-hooking fabric to prevent them from fraying.

2. Enlarge Bird and Flower, opposite, 200% and then transfer it onto your rug backing fabric, referring to page 14 for details on transferring patterns.

3. Cut the wool into size-8 strips (¼" wide) using a strip cutter or your rotary cutter.

4. Using the photograph as a guide, hook the design in the following order:
   - Hook the bird and flower motifs
   - Hook the border by outlining the tongue shapes first and then filling in each tongue.

5. Block the hooked design before assembling the sleeve. See page 18 for details on blocking.

Assembling the Sleeve

All seam allowances are ½" wide unless otherwise stated. Seams are sewn with right sides together. Press the seams open or to one side, whichever seems less bulky, depending on your fabric.

1. Fold the hooked piece in half right sides together along the 42" length. Pin the raw edges together and then seam them together, leaving a 3" opening along the seam line. Lay the piece so the seam is centered along the back and press the seam open.

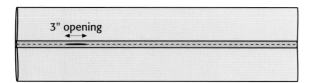

3" opening

2. Stitch each end closed and then turn the sleeve right side out through the opening. Press.

3. On one end of the sleeve, make four horizontal buttonholes, evenly spaced across the end of the sleeve. After the pillow is complete, you can determine the button placement for snug, but not too tight, fit.

Make four evenly-spaced buttonholes on one end.

Making the Pillow

1. From the ⅝ yard of tapestry fabric, cut two pieces, 18½" x 26", for the pillow front and back.

2. Sew the pillow front and back together using a ½" seam. Leave an opening along the top edge at the center of the pillow, for turning and stuffing. Once the sleeve is in place, it will cover the opening.

3. Trim the corners, and then turn the pillow right side out and press. Stuff the pillow and stitch the opening closed.

4. Place the sleeve around the pillow and mark the placement for the buttons. Sew the buttons on the sleeve end and button it onto the pillow.

Stuffing

You can use polyester stuffing in your pillow, or you can be thrifty and use recycled items. The pillow shown is stuffed with two old sweaters, one old dress, small bits of wool, and other fabric scraps. It makes the pillow lumpy and heavy—just like the ones that used to be on the beds at grandma's farm!

Bird and Flower Hooked Rug Pattern
One square = ½".
Enlarge pattern 200% to 10½" x 17½".

Pennies from Heaven

by Janet Carruth

Janet Carruth has found a creative way for using the traditional appliquéd penny shape in this clever lampshade. The lamp is a perfect partner for the little scrap rug that also carries the circle theme. If you've been hooking for a while, you probably have all sorts of wool strips that you could use in the rug project. If not, this will be a fun time to build up your stash of plaids and colors!

Appliquéd Lampshade

A lampshade may seem like an unusual place for a penny rug, but standing tall, this project provides a great showcase for your beautiful wool pennies and really spotlights them when the lamp is turned on.

Finished size: 7½" tall; 10" diameter at bottom; 6" diameter at top

Materials

Wool yardage amounts are based on 60"-wide wool. Wash new wool before using.

⅔ yard of black wool for background

6" x 18" piece of red wool for large pennies

6" x 18" piece of gold wool for small pennies

¼ yard of paper-backed fusible web

2 skeins of red pearl cotton (size 5)

1 skein of golden brown pearl cotton (size 5)

Size 22 chenille needle

Candlestick lamp and lampshade (available at craft stores or discount department stores)

Freezer paper

Newspaper

Black fine-point permanent marker

Chalk wheel or white chalk pencil

Fabric glue

10 to 15 spring-type clothespins

Lampshade Pattern

Because lampshade sizes vary, rather than providing a printed pattern, we have included instructions on how to make a pattern that will fit your particular lampshade.

1. Lay your lampshade on a large piece of paper— newspaper works great.

2. Draw along the top and bottom edge where the shade touches the paper. Roll the shade and continue marking until the shade has rolled one complete turn.

3. Add ½" to one straight edge for an overlap at the back seam.

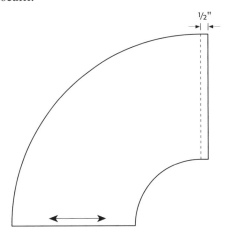

Cutting

Patterns for the appliqué pennies are shown opposite. For this project, Janet used fusible web to make her templates and adhered the pennies to the background fabric for appliqué. If you prefer, you could use freezer-paper templates instead, referring to page 10 for directions.

- Draw 18 large circles onto fusible web. Following the manufacturer's instructions, iron the fusible web onto the red wool. Cut out the circles and remove the paper backing.

- Draw 18 small circles onto fusible web. Iron the web onto the gold wool, cut out the circles and remove the paper backing.

From the black wool, cut:
- 2 strips, 1¼" x width of fabric
- 1 lampshade pattern

Making the Lampshade

1. Lay out the black lampshade wool on a table. Using a chalk wheel or chalk pencil and ruler, mark ½" along both curved edges and across one straight edge of the wool. Trim will cover the chalk marks on the curved edges, while the mark on the straight edge will be covered by the overlapping edges.

2. Place 18 red circles randomly within the unmarked section of the lampshade. Pin the circles in place with a dry iron.

3. Wrap the wool around the shade to check the circle placement. Adjust the circles if necessary. When you are satisfied with their placement, fuse the red circles in place with a dry iron.

4. Appliqué the red circles in place using the red pearl cotton and the blanket stitch. To make the stitches the same size, draw a smaller circle inside the red circle, and stitch to this line.
   Note: The black wool edges are almost completely cut on the bias, so take care not to stretch the lampshade out of shape as you appliqué.

Locking Stitches

Sometimes when doing a blanket stitch around a curve, the thread drops below the edge of the appliqué where it isn't quite visible. To prevent this from happening, Janet recommends using a locking type of stitch, which is often used in making buttonholes by hand. Follow the diagram below to make stitches that form knots at the outside edge of the appliquéd penny, which keeps the thread nice and even along the curved edge.

Make a standard blanket stitch. Bring needle around and back through loop. Pull thread snug.

5. Steam press the lampshade from the wrong side, taking care not to stretch it.

6. Center a small gold circle in each red circle. Fuse in place and blanket stitch using the golden brown pearl cotton, as you did for the red pennies. Steam press again.

7. Place the black wool around the lampshade. Hold it in place with a few clothespins around the top and bottom edges. Lightly glue the overlap in the back. Use the glue sparingly, as too much glue will soak through the fabric and show even after it has dried.

8. Put a few drops of glue under the top and bottom edges of the black wool, taking care to stay within the ½" margins that will be covered by the trim pieces.

9. Press the two 1¼"-wide trim strips in half lengthwise. Open up one strip and place the crease along the bottom edge of the shade so that half is on the front and half is on the inside of the shade. Use clothespins to hold the trim in place. Mark a ½" overlap and trim off the excess fabric.

10. Glue the overlap section and then glue the trim to the inside of the shade. Place a thin bead of glue along the inside edge of the metal ring at the bottom of the shade. Apply another bead of glue closer to the edge of the wool trim. Hold the trim in place with clothespins until the glue has dried.

11. After the glue has dried, on the outside of the lampshade, blanket stitch the black trim in place using red pearl cotton.

12. Repeat steps 9–11 for the trim at the top edge of the lampshade.

Appliqué Patterns
Patterns are full size.
Do not add seam allowances.

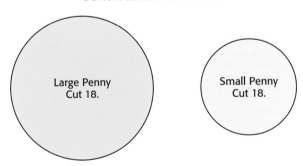

Large Penny
Cut 18.

Small Penny
Cut 18.

Hooked
Penny Rug

Janet Carruth headed to rug camp with a sack of scraps, confident that she'd return with an empty bag and a completed penny rug. Once there, instructor Patsy Becker inspired her to transform her idea into a more complex design that just happened to require more fabrics. The rug is a delight, but Janet's scrap bag is still filled to overflowing!

Finished size: 19" x 13"

Materials

Wool yardage amounts are based on 60"-wide wool. Wash new wool before using. Amounts allow for four times the area that will be hooked.

½ yard total of assorted dark gray and black wool for background and outside edge

½ yard total of assorted scraps or leftover strips, including plaids, herringbones, and solids for quarter circle sections

24" x 30" piece of backing fabric (linen, monk's cloth, or Scottish burlap)

Black permanent marker

Ruler

Hooking the Rug

1. Using a permanent marker and a ruler, draw a 12" x 18" rectangle centered on the backing fabric.

2. Divide the rectangle into a grid of 3" squares; six squares across and three squares down.

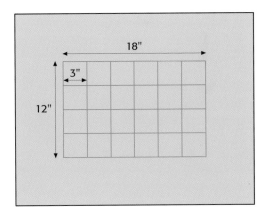

3. Draw a 3"-diameter circle inside each square by using a compass or the pattern below. Then draw more grid lines, dividing the 3" squares in half both horizontally and vertically to create divided circles.

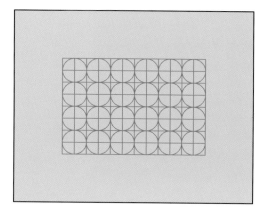

4. Cut the wool into size 8 strips (¼" wide) using a strip cutter or your rotary cutter.

5. Hook the rug in the following order:

   ◆ Hook the lines bisecting the circles.

   ◆ Hook the quarter-circle sections. Fill some sections with one color of wool and others with two different colors for a scrappier look. If desired, you can outline the circles in one color and fill in the area with a different color.

   ◆ Hook the background areas in the squares using the assorted black strips. Mix up the strips for a random look that will give your rug added depth and texture.

   ◆ Hook two rows of black around the outside edge of the mat.

Finishing the Rug

This rug is finished by turning the backing fabric to the back of the rug and whipstitching it into place. For complete details on this type of edge finish, please see "Finishing Details" on page 18. You'll also find instructions for other options for finishing your rug.

1. Block the rug. Lay it on a flat surface, such as your ironing board, cover it with a wet towel, and press the towel with the iron to steam the rug. If the rug is at all out of square, gently pull it back into shape and allow the damp rug to dry overnight.

2. Bind the rug using your desired method.

3. Sign and date your rug. You may sign your name with an indelible pen along the edge of the backing fabric on the back of the rug, or you can make a fabric label and hand stitch it to the back of your rug.

4. Use a black permanent marker to blacken any foundation fabric that shows around the edge of the rug from the front side.

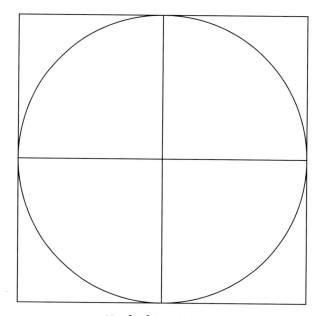

Hooked Rug Pattern
3" Circle and Square
Pattern is full size.

Resources

Your local quilt shop or fabric store is likely to be a good source of the supplies you'll need for making a penny rug or hooked rug. However, if you want to expand your supplies beyond the basics, you may want to refer to one or more of the sources listed below for strip cutters, rug-hooking frames, wools, and dyes.

Blackberry Primitives
1944 High St.
Lincoln, NE 68502
402-421-1361
402-423-8464
www.blackberryprimitives.com
A large selection of overdyed and textured wools, plus necessary tools

Braid Aid
PO Box 603
Pembroke, MA 02359
781-826-6091
www.braid-aid.com
Tools and supplies for rug hooking

The Dorr Mill Store
PO Box 88
Guild, NH 03754
800-846-DORR
www.dorrmillstore.com
Mill-direct wools in solids and textures

Harry M. Fraser Company
PO Box 939
Stoneville, NC 27048
336-573-9830
www.fraserrugs.com
Bliss and Fraser strip cutters

Kindred Spirits
115 Colonial La.
Kettering, OH 45429
937-435-7758
www.kindredspiritsdesigns.com
Hand-dyed wools and yarn, dyeing supplies, and tools for rug hooking and appliquéing

Rigby Precision Products
PO Box 158
Bridgton, ME 04009
207-647-5679
Rigby strip cutters

Speckled Hen Country Store
915 First St., Ste. A
Snohomish, WA 98290
360-568-9758
Hand-dyed wools, Cushing dyes, decorative items

W. Cushing & Company
PO Box 351
Kennebunkport, ME 04046
800-626-7847
www.wcushing.com
Dyes and supplies for overdyeing wool

The Wool Studio
706 Brownsville Rd.
Sinking Spring, PA 19608
610-678-5448
www.thewoolstudio.com
Large supply of "as-is" wools

About the Designers

Janet Carija Brandt

Janet is the author of the book that started the whole wool appliqué phenomenon: *WOW! Wool on Wool Folk Art Quilts.* In addition to designing for Moda Fabrics, Janet is combining her love of handwork and folk art with the miracles of machine embroidery and personal digitizing. Visit her Web site at www.carijarts.com.

Janet Carruth

Cofounder of the Quilted Apple quilt shop in Phoenix, Arizona, Janet no longer owns the shop but has actively taught classes there since selling her share of the business to partner Laurene Sinema in 1985. Janet began designing projects for rug-hooking classes at the shop, and penny-rug classes soon followed. Janet self-published *Design Originals,* a book of rug-hooking patterns in 1994, and later collaborated with Laurene on the book *Weathered Vanes* for Red Wagon Publishing that features quilts and hooked projects.

Kindred Spirits

A shared joy of expressing themselves through their creations and a shared appreciation of all things that have a "loved-for-a-long-time" look inspired Sally Korte and Alice Strebel to begin a business that has brought them national recognition and a loyal following. Kindred Spirits' designs have been featured in numerous national publications, and the company enjoys the reputation of being unique and original. Sally and Alice are involved in lecturing and teaching nationally as well as internationally and they consider themselves motivational speakers on the topic of personal creativity. For more information about their shop, patterns, books, wool, and other supplies, visit their Web site at www.kindredspiritsdesigns.com.

Little Quilts

Little Quilts is the combined talents and efforts of Alice Berg, Mary Ellen Von Holt, and Sylvia Johnson. Located in Marietta, Georgia, they have been design-ing projects for small quilts in a traditional style since 1986. Authors of *Little Quilts All Through the House, Celebrate with Little Quilts, Living with Little Quilts,* and *Patriotic Little Quilts,* and fabric designers for Peter Pan Fabrics, these women have made the name Little Quilts recognizable worldwide. Currently they own a retail store located in a restored corn mill in Marietta. For more information about their store, designs, and publications, visit their Web site at www.littlequilts.com.

Sew Unique Creations

Tara Lynn Darr founded her company in 1999 when she decided it would be nice to stay at home with her three small children, yet she needed to earn an income. Today she has a pattern line of over 200 designs that include quilts, penny rugs, hooked rugs, pillows, and doll patterns, and she has self-published two books, *A View Through My Window* and *Pennyrugs and Pillow Thangs.* Sew Unique Creations has been steadily growing, so you can look for new patterns on the company's Web site at www.sewuniquecreations.com.

Whimsicals

Whimsicals is a mother (Jackie Conaway) and daughter (Terri Degenkolb) team who share a love for quilting and creating. They've merged Jackie's more traditional side with Terri's doodles to create the age-worn, primitive look that they both love. Together they have published numerous books and patterns as well as fabric lines for A.E. Nathan. To see other books and patterns by Whimsicals, visit their Web site at www.whimsicals.biz.

Tonee White

Tonee has been quilting for more than a dozen years and has written several books published by Martingale & Company, all featuring her appliquilt technique that combines appliquéing and quilting in one step. She teaches and lectures nationally, and from time to time her designs can be found in quilt-ing magazines. In addition to quilting and appliquéing, Tonee is an avid rug hooker and is presently working on coordinating quilts and rugs for the home. Tonee lives in Scottsdale, Arizona, with her husband, Bob, and two of their seven children.